AMAZING GRACE

*STORIES OF LESBIAN
AND GAY FAITH*

EDITED BY
MALCOLM BOYD
AND NANCY L. WILSON

The Crossing Press
Freedom, CA 95019

Library of Congress Cataloging-in-Publication Data

Amazing Grace: stories of lesbian and gay faith / edited by
   Malcolm Boyd and Nancy L. Wilson.
   p. cm.
   Includes bibliographical references.
   ISBN 0-89594-480-4   ISBN 0-89594-479-0 (pbk.)
   1. Gays--Religious life. 2. Gays--United States--Biography.
   I. Boyd, Malcolm, 1923- . II. Wilson, Nancy L., 1950- .
BV4596.G38A43 1991   91-23932
208'.664--dc20   CIP

Contents

INTRODUCTION

Lesbian and gay Christians are everywhere—in the arts and academia, sports and the military, politics and the professions. We co-exist with lesbians and gay men who are Jews, Buddhists, Muslims and New Age followers.

We know at firsthand the church's beauty and cruelty, its sacramental grace and homophobic sins, its healing and dis-ease, its discipleship of Christ and betrayal of Christ, its warm expression of God's love and cold repudiation of God's love.

This book comprises storytelling. While our stories share external similarities, our individual experiences remain widely different. In the personal stories that follow, you will discover our spiritual pilgrimages, childhood experiences, mature relationships, sexual awakening, grappling with faith, encounters with social justice and our confrontations with AIDS. Let us share with you the inner and outer journeys of our lives as lesbian and gay Christians.

Malcolm Boyd and Nancy L. Wilson

MALCOLM BOYD

Underground Christians

Burnt-out people
    play with fire again
    light candles in darkness
    moral minority emerges
    integrates diversity
    feminine, masculine
    hetero, gay, lesbian
    black, white
    Latino, Anglo
    European, Asian, African
    new breed
    sophisticated beyond belief
    innocent as lambs
    tough survivors, tender lovers

God isn't Lionel Barrymore anymore
    glimmer of deity
    along lines of
    Dorothy Day, Barbara Jordan
    Eleanor Roosevelt, Georgia O'Keeffe

Endless procession
    chanting, robed
    women and men
    (a place for me)
    here, tiny seashell
    on floor of mighty sea
    there, small streak of color
    in blazing sunset

*A*s a speaker at the 1967 meeting of the Division of Christian Education of the National Council of Churches in Dallas, I first reported that a new Christian movement which I called the underground church was cutting across the denominational lines and rapidly spreading throughout the nation, "bypassing official structures and leadership."

This movement began with a tiny, committed group of men and women and, I noted, was "forcing changes on the church from the middle and the bottom." I went on to explain that about six months before, I first became aware of an underground church which was beginning to express spiritual power among people. Existing ecumenical agencies had helped to foster and nurture this groundswell, but they had become too official and inflexible. What I was talking about had already happened in the "basement" of these structures. The New York Times, Time, and national television quickly began to investigate the new movement.

I described the people of this underground: "Some go to church and some don't. Those who do are deeply frustrated by existing forms and attitudes, by the ungiving nature of the official church. The movement is deeply concerned about human need. Its religious questions are about poverty, race, sexuality, war and peace—but with emphasis on doing, not talking."

Soon I encountered the underground church in many different places. Once, in a Chicago suburban home when I was asked to concelebrate the eucharist with a married Roman Catholic priest for a group of Catholic women, men and children. Again, inside a huge, shadowy Episcopal cathedral at night when I stood before a candle-lit altar in a catacomb-like setting, surrounded by lesbians and gay men engaged in the eucharist. Today the underground church can still be found in many places, including the Christian movement within the world of lesbians and gay men. A lesbian/gay spirituality and theology is emerging out of the experience of gay people. It is something to be mined, not discovered, exists in gay consciousness, and takes concrete form in storytelling.

For gays, God's revelation is a continuing process in life; not locked inside, or restricted to, the pages of the Bible. It stands with feminist theology in invoking a new "theology of the church." This veers sharply away from institutional patriarchy. A monarchial, rigid type of church leadership needs to be supplanted by a collegial form which is more democratic and reflects an open community. The church has no right to place the perpetuation of its own power and machinery over the struggles and needs of people. As priest-theologian Carter Heyward said at a Feminist Liberation Theology conference, "None of our stories are solos....No more crucifixions. God is with us in our vulnerability."

The Christian movement in the gay and lesbian world is tiny but strong.

If it can address a spiritual hunger that is universal, and focus on Christ's gospel instead of simply its own problems, it may exert a profound influence on the course of Christianity in America.

It knows the meaning of persecution from experience. Can it proclaim the crucified and risen Christ in fresh, compelling ways to the whole church, the whole society? Can the movement find wide expression as a "moral minority" of genuine spiritual integrity and witnessing power?

One major challenge for the gay and lesbian Christian movement is to make a prophetic Christian witness in the arena of mass media and exploitation. We live, move and have our being in the Age of Hype. Critic Louis Kronenberger noted that, "the only man fit to be compared with Sigmund Freud or Karl Marx is P. T. Barnum." The king of circus enterprises relied heavily on a barrage of publicity, stunts, sensational gimmicks and unhampered tub-thumping. We've come to televangelists, packaged religion and God in prime time.

Billy Graham said in an interview in 1955: "I am selling the greatest product in the world; why shouldn't it be promoted as well as soap?" Product? If the gospel of Jesus Christ is truly on a par with soap, exploitation might seem to be in order. But exploitation is a mortal sin when it perceives people as objects, faces in a crowd, statistics for sales or conversions, and uses them for venal purposes. Gay people know what it is like to be perceived as objects; we understand how it feels to be members of the lonely crowd.

Jesus Christ, far from exploiting the political and cultural situation in which he found himself, refused temptations of worldly power, defused a passion of adulation present in crowds that hailed him, and willed to die in a setting of apparent humiliation and defeat. He provided the refutation, as well as the antithesis, of exploitation. His conduct represents the meaning of love on a vast public, as well as an intensely personal, scale.

The mainstream Christian church has encumbered itself with bigness, respectability over radical truth, and preaching cultural conformity in place of Christ's gospel of unconditional love.

In the past, exploitation of people for Jesus Christ was carried out by swords, gold, guns and flags. Yet this same Jesus Christ emptied himself of power for the sake of humankind. Gay people can identify with this power-lessness, and God's love rooted in it. To cleanse itself, the church needs to stress servanthood over success, humility over secular power, and the simple witness of its own "emptiness" in faithful response to God's uncalculated, freely offered gift of wholeness for all conditions of people.

Can an underground church of lesbian and gay Christians pursue a course of discipleship to honor Christ's cross and "convert" churchianity to true servanthood in Christ's name? Can this movement hear Christ's call in humility and move into the world to do foot-washing and healing?

This is a specific place for the gay and lesbian Christian movement to make an honest, costly witness. Here is a challenge which will enable the movement to distance itself from conventional religion and take a stand for ethical truth. This is a way to de-ghettoize itself. Let me explain. There is a need for gay and lesbian spirituality to find expression in its own liturgies, prayers and music; its particularity should be finely honed. Yet in meaning and service in Christ's name it must move out of narrowness into the mainstream. Does the movement want to do this? Time will tell.

Gay and lesbian spirituality will suffer irremediably, and no doubt vanish as a serious entity on the religious horizon, if it doesn't care for the poor, homeless, suffering, and disenfranchised outside its own parameters. AIDS is leading it to a close, deep identification with the crucified and risen Christ, who calls the gay and lesbian Christian movement to the way of the cross instead of becoming yet another religious success myth.

As gay people, we affirm that the deep hunger and passionate yearning for wholeness—coming home within oneself and community—is sacred. Our wholeness includes our God-given sexuality; we share this with all other people. We offer thanks for this as a form of bonding, mutual support, shared pleasure, and spiritual fulfillment.

British writer Edward Carpenter perceived early in this century that the "real significance of the homosexual temperament" is that "the non-warlike man and the undomestic woman...sought new outlets for their energies...different occupations," especially in "the arts and crafts, spirituality, shamanism and priesthood." I learned Carpenter was right when I discovered in the '60s that other gay people like myself found self-realization and service to others in the church, the civil rights movement, and the peace movement. On an early Freedom ride in 1961, and in numerous demonstrations and jail cells in the North and South, I was with gay and lesbian companions.

The *zeitgeist* of that period changed gay history. Civil rights in the U.S. matched liberation movements elsewhere in the world; liberation theology and black theology appeared. The feminist movement emerged as a wellspring of original, forceful, fresh thought. Post-modernism, process thought, and creation-centered spirituality confronted an outworn, tired, casuistical theology with a new spirit that is radical.

Gay spirit, the foundation of gay social action in the world, is not a mysterious thing to pinpoint. It emerges from gay sensibilities. As lesbian poet Judy Grahn writes: "There are gay countercultures, undergrounds, circles, cliques, ghettos, histories and sensibilities. How do I know when a sensibility is gay? Because gay people gather round it and sense it and project it and act it out." Out of our experience as gay people evolves our belief system, our faith, the kind of spiritual and religious impulses we share, our sense of relationship to God, and stemming from this, our commitment to social action and fidelity to justice issues.

How could gay people not recognize God at work in the struggles of the oppressed for liberation? We are a wounded people who bear scars. Our experience has been one of oppression, hiddenness, and risk, combined with tenacity, courage, adaptation and a sense of irony. One's job could crumble in an instant of public accusation or disclosure; so could parental support, social standing or a roof over one's head. The ghetto was both salvific and a snake pit. Self-hatred and absence of self-esteem radiated outward to become virulent homophobia. No positive role models were permitted. The burden was sometimes made even heavier if one went to a church or a synagogue in search of solace or strength, and found rejection and denunciation. No wonder Judy Garland became a gay goddess. She was down, too. Her song of heartbreak became ours. She placed her hope "over the rainbow."

Gay spirit is open to diverse intellectual and theological input. As a gay man, I have learned in years of Jungian dream therapy how I am engaged upon my "individuation process." From Zen Buddhism, I am instructed to confront problems now—or they may await me, again and again, in the future. Christianity tells me I can claim the freely offered gift of new life, which includes deep involvement and true sharing with others, or I can choose the "hell" of isolation because I opt to remain solitary and in control.

My intimate connection with AIDS has taught me that we cannot exist in the past or future. Our consciousness of time needs to be transformed. In gay spirit, the present has a quality of sacredness. The present moment contains an urgency, both personally and socially, to act. The time we share with God and each other is now.

An example of this emerged not long ago when I visited Michael, a young man with AIDS, in Los Angeles. His lover was away at work. Michael lay on a cot in the living room of their apartment. He was very weak and tired. I pulled up a chair and placed it next to the cot, but Michael asked me to sit alongside him. He drew himself up to a sitting position and we held hands until he asked me to hold him in my arms. Michael asked me two direct questions: "Does God love me?" "Yes," I replied. "Where am I going after I die?" Michael asked. "You will be in a continuing life with God after you die," I replied.

We talked for a long while. As I left, Michael said, "Will you come back the same time next week?" I allowed as how I would. Three days later, however, Michael died. There's no extra time, I learned once again. How can we help one another along the way, maybe with a symbolic reminder of God's love expressed in human terms? Can we help to raise one another's self-esteem a notch in a world that likes to batter it? Become a concrete expression of compassion in the midst of terror, fear and hate?

"If we could but recognize our common humanity, that we do belong together, that our destinies are bound up with one another's, that we can be free only together, that we can be human only together...." These are Desmond M. Tutu's words at his installation as Archbishop of Cape Town. He was speaking, of course, in the context of the possibilities of "a glorious South Africa...where all live harmoniously as members of one family, the human family, God's family."

His words also speak sensitively and prophetically in our society in the context of where, and how, gay people fit. "If we could but recognize our common humanity...." We cannot do this when some of us, lesbians and gay men, are likened to lepers or notorious sinners by many noted and respected religious leaders because of our sexual orientation. Why does anti-gay prejudice and hatred continue to be so virulent and negative a force in mainstream Christianity?

I'm beginning to sense the shape of the answer: Can it be that many people, however reasonable they think they are, in fact are emotionally trapped by a stereotype of gay men and lesbians? It is conditioned by a spiritually literalistic, anti-intellectual, anti-spiritual and tragically fundamentalistic comprehension of scripture.

The stereotype does not fit.

We gays—many of whom can be found Sunday mornings in a nearby pew in a neighborhood church—work in business, government, academia, the media, religion, sports. We do volunteer work, teach school, practice law and medicine, cut lawns and cook meals; we report the news, say Mass, preach sermons, and serve in the armed forces; we play tennis and cards, watch TV and grouse about the freeway. We live up the street, or next door. (If you look closely, maybe you'll find one of us living in your home.)

Since much of gay identity remains closeted, largely due to homophobia rooted in religious prejudice and hatred, co-workers in our places of employment frequently do not identify us as gays. Neither do many mothers and fathers, even wives and husbands. But organized religion needs to comprehend and acknowledge who gays are and what contributions we make to society. Conscious awareness of an experienced human relationship between gays and non-gays is needed if there is to be an equivalent development of communication and respect. And rights.

There are analogies. Jewish stereotypes, buried deep in the hatred of anti-Semitism, lose potency in one-on-one contact that contradicts them. Black stereotypes diminish in intensity when people are given an opportunity to interact as themselves, not figments of myth or imagination.

Honesty and openness, and mutual respect, let in the fresh air of hope, and seem much closer to the meaning of Christ's gospel than untruths and hiddenness. If hypocrisy and lies hold the day, that hope cannot be realized. The circle of hatred and self-hatred draws murderously tighter. A majority of gay people, fearful of condemnation, choose to remain hidden. This plays into the hands of those who perpetuate the stereotype of homosexuality.

However, we have had enough of social and private lies. Liberation from any form of past repression surely has to include, for all of us, the freedom to become one's self. This seems integral to the meaning of the Exodus in the Old Testament and Christ's crucifixion and resurrection in the New Testament.

One of the contributions that we gays can make to contemporary spirituality is a celebration of diversity vis-à-vis sameness or conformity for its own sake. This is why false, rigid stereotypes of gay uniformity are so ironic, misleading and absurd. The gay and lesbian population is astounding in its diversity. We are thin and fat, old and young, dark and blond, attractive and ugly, sexy and asexual, rubes and sophisticates, puritans and libertines, rural and urban, Latino and white and black and Asian, Christians and Jews and New Age and Muslims and atheists. And we lack easily identifiable outward marks, the cliché limp wrist notwithstanding.

To change public consciousness about gay reality will not be easy. There are several obstacles: The most obvious public one is religious. It is the current messianic movement of biblical fundamentalism-cum-politics, Khomeini-like in severity and disproportionately well-financed, which is attempting to subvert the Constitution and link church and state through punitive legislation, much of it aimed at gays.

It required "black power," the concentrated effort by African-Americans to assert self-acceptance and pride in the face of rejection and contempt, to change both blacks' and whites' attitudes toward blackness. I remember Rosa Parks, who prepared the way for Dr. Martin Luther King, Jr.'s leadership, reflecting on her refusal to sit in the back of a bus in Alabama, recalling "the appalling silence of the good people."

As a gay Christian, I wonder where are the silent "good people"— including the "good," still-hidden gay people and the "good" Christians flocking to the churches—who will come forward in response to Christ's unconditional love to advance the cause of gay peoples' rights?

Ours is by no means the first age in which gay men and lesbians have struggled in a highly particular way with prejudice rooted in religion and with questions of faith, spirit, and theology. Yet the relationship between gay people and organized religion has long been an ambiguous, even a tortured one. Gay people have for time immemorial virtually honeycombed the church, its machinery and inner working. Lesbians and gay men have filled convents and monasteries for generations. Gay folk have sat on bishops' thrones (and continue to do so), celebrated liturgies, preached the Word, taught in the church's schools, composed and performed the church's music. The church, despite its institutional homophobia, seemed a more likely place for gays to inhabit than, say, the military. Inside the church we would be with a large number of other brothers and sisters, even if occupying closets. And, one has the drama and beauty of the liturgy, the high intellectual life of theology, candlelight and color and incense, music to stir the senses, a lively balance between things immanent and transcendent.

The year was 1938 and I was in high school. Homosexual? Gay? I had only the vaguest idea what these words meant. Maleness was a homoerotic mystery to me. I seemed detached from life, looking on, trying to figure out essential meanings.

Once, I visited a house where two young men sat in an upstairs bedroom at night. One was naked, the other wore jockey shorts. The door of their room was open. I watched them talk and laugh, horse around good-naturedly. I yearned to be with them and to possess their naturalness and freedom. What I saw gave me an erotic image as sharp as an electric shock.

I dated girls and loved to go dancing with them, but had no erotic interest in them at all. I remember the most breathtakingly beautiful boy I knew in school. He was perfect, a prince with bold, madly hot eyes and a Prince Valiant's magnificent body. When he stood close to me, looked into my eyes and placed his hand on my shoulder, my face burned. My eyes must have revealed my desire to roll naked with him on the bare ground and devour his body. He invited me to share his car for a double-date to a school dance. I can't remember the girls at all. I longed to run my hands over his naked body, kiss his pliant warm lips, feel absolutely free to roam wantonly over the verdant hills and lush valleys of his physical continent.

However, I was utterly petrified. Every morning meant a fresh incursion as a hidden, innocent gay boy, into an alien environment in which I did not belong and must play a role. I hated my clothes, didn't want to wear them, felt (correctly) that they didn't express "me." My clothes were correct, proper, binding; I wanted to be wild, free, bohemian. I couldn't stand the way I looked and felt as a prisoner cooped up. I yearned to be my gorgeous, sensuous, ineffably liberated self whom I saw only sporadically behind a mirror, and whom no one else ever caught a glimpse of. Deep inside, I wanted to get out.

I started to run around with three other boys who were outsiders like me. John's parents were adamantly puritanical, bitter, joyless and plodding. John, on the other hand, was a blithe spirit trying to get out of his inherited imprisonment to express himself. He had a wild side, an absolutely mad sense of humor and play. Occasionally, this would show. One afternoon, I remember we were alone and unzipped our pants, got our peckers out and felt each other's. They got hard. John blushed. We felt awkward and unsafe sitting in his parents' living room. What if they came home and walked in on us? We got our penises back in our pants and zipped up.

John and I shared a lot of feelings. I understand now that both of us were gay kids. It would have been marvelous to be able to share that. But we were molded by the times we were living in and our own upbringing, and the repression of gay instincts and feelings. A few years later, in World War II, John died in a naval accident in the South Pacific.

Whitney was another member of our youthful circle. He was gay, too, I realize. Whitney was exuberant, larger than life, witty, acerbic, eccentric, uncontrollable. He made everyone laugh because he was simply outrageous. No one could ever get close to Whitney, so although we spent a lot of time together in our foursome, I couldn't either. One Sunday afternoon in his room at his family's expensive home, Whitney put a gun in his mouth and blew his head off. He left no note or explanation.

The fourth member of our high school group of friends was not a gay boy, yet ironically he seems (as I look back) the gayest of us all. He had the most eccentric sense of humor, acted out even more than the rest, and was every bit as much an outsider.

A fifth boy tried briefly to join our group. He had a dark side like Batman. Ralph looked sensual in his tight black pants, wore a sardonic grin, was outwardly a very physical man at home in his body, and expressed a desire to get sexy with us. We just didn't know how to respond. Strip down and have group sex? He scared and fascinated us at the same time.

One Sunday afternoon we were driving around the city, all five of us, when he announced the rest of the boys should take my clothes off and play with me. It was all so sudden. The others grabbed me. I resented Ralph's commanding role in our easy comradeship. A slow, horny night of strip poker might have turned me on and given me permission to get into sex with the others. But being earmarked for seeming rape inside the car pushed my storm signals. I decided my pants were damned well going to come off only when I wanted them to. I nearly wrecked the back seat of the car in determination to protect my virginity or, at least, keep my pants on.

After that incident, Ralph vanished abruptly. A few years later, I heard he had gone to a prestigious university, joined the most elite fraternity, and introduced S/M and raw sex into its initiation rites for pledges. He was summarily thrown out and, the last I knew, was a bartender at a chic country club and the lover of the heir to one of America's great fortunes.

If my sexual awakening was slow, except for hot, regular masturbation, my religious experience was a rapidly unfolding one. I sang in the choir until my voice changed. And, I became an acolyte serving at the altar. Each Sunday I attended the regular 11 a.m. church service as well as Sunday

School. Many evenings I went to church supper meetings.

While women served on the Altar Guild, raised money and prepared church suppers, the priestly side of church life was a masculine preserve. Priests whom I now realize were closeted homosexuals wore tight masks. Theirs was a mysterious world that I identified with caustic criticism, brittle laughter, a veneer of sophistication and a never-ending charade in which manners paraded relentlessly. Usually I saw them wearing long black cassocks, silver crosses dangling around their necks.

I knew Jesus was sexless, of course. The Virgin Birth underscored this. In my view, it would have approached blasphemy and exceeded poor taste to even imagine Mary and Joseph engaged in physical passion. She was eternally pure. Purity meant sexual abstinence. Although Jesus was a man living on earth for what they said was thirty-three years, he appeared to be super man: idealistic, self-sacrificing, perfectly poised, reflective, active in good causes, always reasonable and loving. It was inconceivable to me that he could ever have succumbed to the weakness of being human in a sexual way. It was crazy to think of Jesus in such an undignified position. And, the mere suggestion of his being out of control and passionate made me feel guilty for holding dirty thoughts. I knew I was a victim of dirty thoughts when I got a hard-on in bed, rubbed my erect cock against the sheets until I shot my cum. How could I be saved? How could I, like Jesus, overcome my terrible weakness, rigidly control my humanity and become holy?

Forty years later, as an Episcopal priest and author of a best-selling book of prayers, I sat in a Toronto television studio taping an interview. The interviewer got on the subject of Jesus's humanity. It appeared to be an obsession with him. Posing as a hard-bitten cynic and critic of the church, he seemed consumed by questions of faith.

What did I mean that Jesus became fully human? Well, I said, I mean that he had a head, shoulders, chest, stomach, a penis, legs and feet. The interview continued on its way. But when it was seen a few weeks later on national television, an uproar ensued about my remark. Dozens of angry phone calls reached the media and church authorities. One person called an Anglican bishop and wrathfully exclaimed: "Jesus did not have a penis!"

He did. This is simply a natural premise drawn from the Incarnation itself, the church's teaching that Jesus Christ, the Son of God, was also fully human in his thirty-three years. Inescapably, then, he was sexual.

Always I seemed to understand this. Yet accepting my own sexuality, and relating it to my spirituality, seemed almost impossible.

After I graduated from college and went to work in Hollywood, there were no gay role models, magazines or newspapers. Gay wasn't even a word I heard: homosexual was. Queer was. Faggot was. I knew these words well.

Once a young magazine editor for whom I wrote film reviews invited me for drinks at a residential hotel where he lived. He asked me to spend the night with him. I yearned to do this. But I panicked. Wouldn't this be admitting I was like that? Wasn't it better just to remain alone, lonely and impersonal? Or, participate in a tough macho scene with a stranger who resembled a fantasy, get my rocks off, and get the hell out like a man? Yet I was dying to share tenderly with the young editor, laugh and cry and be myself. However, leaving him alone there, I went home and masturbated. I was a man. I had protected my masculinity.

My search for love and wholeness I wrote about in my book *Look Back in Joy*. Loneliness pursued me as if it were a pack of wolves; my body and soul remained polarized. They were enemies.

One morning I awoke with a hangover in a strange hotel room. Looking out the window, I saw it was snowing. The day was gray and white. I simply had no idea where I was going in my life. I was terrified. The universe seemed akin to that room: devoid of character, personality or warmth. I seemed trapped in a set for Sartre's *No Exit.*

As gay people, we need to create fresh, new theological insights rooted in our own gay experience. As I wrote in Mark Thompson's *Gay Spirit: Myth and Meaning*, "We are a broken people who understand the brokenness of others."

God possesses the wholeness and fullness of what we understand to be body and soul. I expanded on this in *Take Off the Masks*: "This completeness incorporates all of femininity and masculinity. God knows intimately what are our needs of body and soul. Creation is not a distant, impersonal action. Soul is neither superior to body nor can it be separated from it. Because of my belief, I feel assurance and pride in my body and soul. God's honesty and openness let me be honest and open. The experience of loving sexuality brings me closer to God and also to other people. The common clay of creation, the commonality of flesh, blood, desire, and fulfillment, make me grateful to God for all creation...God is experienced in orgasm as much as in inspiring scenes of nature, human friendships, meditations, religious rituals, and acts of charity."

We gay people have a need to seek genuine, deep intimacy with a partner because a gay relationship/extended family quite often has to provide most of the nurture for itself. It is frequently denied sanction and warm, loving support from partners' nuclear families, local church, business associates and immediate neighbors. Whenever a church refuses to bless committed gay relationships, it attacks their stability by refusing at least one measure of societal-religious support. It also denies a sign of the love of God to those who need and ask for it.

I share my life with a gay male partner, Mark Thompson. I want the spiritual as well as the sexual content of our life together to be understood and celebrated by those who misunderstand and oppose us. As a Christian and a priest, I want the church's support in place of its antagonism and judgment. I find that Mark's and my sacramental-and-ordinary times together are not unlike those of many others who live in long-term, committed, loving relationships—in both nuclear and extended families. In such moments, non-verbal as well as verbal vows are expressed, repeated and strengthened.

One such moment we spend together is when we sit down quietly and share conversation at the end of a work-filled, stressful day. It is a moment of communion. We meet each other once again in a fresh, open, vulnerable, sharing way. I hear about Mark's day at his office—on the phone, dealing with people, situations, sometimes crises; and he hears about mine. It is a brief but psychologically valuable unloading time when the day's luggage gets put away. I remember once, after Mark had recounted a particularly hectic incident from his day's work, he looked at me and said, "If I can't tell you about it, whom can I tell?" Precisely.

A special sacramental-and-ordinary moment is that of hugging and holding each other in bed just before falling to sleep. It is nurturing and healing beyond words.

There is also the morning ritual. The alarm clock emits a sharp sound rather like that of a crash accompanying a seven-point quake. I reach out, push the button, turn it off. I reflect a moment, look through the large window over our bed at the brightening sky. Mark stirs at the alarm but does not wake up. His face wears its usual early morning expression of angelic, peaceful innocence.

I get up, unlock the front door, grab the morning paper, walk into the kitchen, start the coffee, sit down in the breakfast nook to read about political scandals, terrorists, basketball scores and new movies. Mark cheerfully appears, pours a cup of coffee, gives me a brush of his lips against mine and picks up a section of the paper.

A new day has begun. I am grateful that Mark shares it with me—casually chatting about some stories in the news, making future plans, just being there. We are partners. God knows, it is a form of grace for us to be happily and creatively together instead of solitary; a rich blessing to be sharers of a common road that intersects our individual paths.

I will shortly celebrate my sixty-eighth birthday, have been an ordained Episcopal priest thirty-five years, and am grateful for my loving and creative relationship with Mark that is going on seven years. "Coming out" for me was a "born again" epiphany that would shock a Jerry Falwell or Pat Robertson by its sheer honest and spiritual intensity. I am grateful for my spirit and focus as a gay man; for my sensitivity, vulnerability, inner strength, being an outsider—even when I'm an insider—seeing and sensing things quite differently.

As gay and lesbian Christians, where do we go from here? The plague of AIDS is a catalyst that confronts all of us with decision-making. Too often, churches have done too little, too late, and sometimes virtually nothing about confronting the plague and helping persons with AIDS. AIDS-related deaths are increasing. Churches are forced to become involved in this struggle—and indeed, in the full arena of human life—in costly, sacrificial ways, or else accept a status as irrelevant.

A favorite story of mine, told by Consuelo Vanderbilt Balsan in her book The Glitter and the Gold, concerns a young American woman's visit to the Austrian imperial court of the Emperor Franz Joseph. She had married an English duke, so was accorded a seat of honor from which she viewed an annual re-enactment of Jesus's washing of the disciples' feet. In this ritual, the Emperor prepared to wash the feet of twelve beggars.

She wrote: "Originally intended as an act of humility, it had become, when I saw it, a scene of splendor in which arrogance masqueraded in spurious simplicity. Twelve of the oldest and poorest men in Vienna were seated on a bench just in front of the tribune from which...I watched the scene. They had been carefully washed and scented so that no unpleasant odor should offend the Imperial nostrils. I was told that on one occasion such precautions had been neglected and that the Emperor at the time had been nearly overcome as he knelt to wash the filthy feet extended to him. The feet now were faultlessly clean—one might almost say manicured—and each man in turn placed a foot in perfumed water. When the Emperor reached the last man, he raised his weary eyes in which I saw disillusion shine cold and bleak. Then rising he returned to the archdukes, who were dressed in gorgeous uniforms and stood in line facing us....It saddened me that an act of Christian humility such as the washing of the beggars' feet should have become an operatic scene shorn of all spiritual meaning."

Jesus's washing of the disciples' feet is a startling and profound example for Christians, showing us how to serve other people's needs and work for peace and justice in the world. Clearly, churches must make a choice: either to stay locked inside stained-glass museums or else move courageously into the mainstream of God's world, risking prestige and respectability in order to represent Christ.

I ran headlong into such a choice in Los Angeles in June, 1990. The County Board of Supervisors met on Tuesdays in their downtown building. They had not provided needed funds and services to deal with AIDS. This, despite the fact that countless more lives were threatened, especially in the African-American and Hispanic communities.

The Los Angeles Coalition for Compassion asked clergy to engage in a prayerful "kneel-in" act of civil disobedience at a Supervisors meeting, to pinpoint the need and bring it more forcefully to the attention of these authorities. Dozens of clergy representing all denominations were asked to take part. Five did.

I did partly from a remembrance of the significance of civil disobedience in the civil rights and peace movements. I was jailed in both northern and southern U.S. jails in the early '60s, heeding the Macedonian call of Martin Luther King, Jr., and twice in Washington, D.C. for participating in peace masses inside the Pentagon.

Let me explain: I never "wanted" to take such a risk, subject myself to the rather overwhelming scrutiny of the combined media, or put up with the utter inconvenience and pain of a jail experience. Yet I responded, from way down in my conscience, to the role models of Gandhi and King. And to the sheer human need represented. There is, at certain significant moments, a necessity for people within the Establishment, representing it, to join hands with those outside it for the cause of Christ's love and justice.

This time I was older. My sixty-seventh birthday came just four days before. I was not so sure of my inner strengths and levels of resistance. It seemed the time to test them again.

On the morning of June twelfth, seven people who were prepared to be arrested (including the five clergy) entered the Supervisors building, accompanied by a support group. Following the invocation and pledge of allegiance to the flag, the seven of us moved forward in the chamber and read a prayer. It said, in part: "We pray that these five Supervisors may this day be moved to hear the cries of the 112,000 persons with HIV disease in this community, whose lives are in their hands." When another Supervisor exclaimed angrily, "This demonstration must cease," Supervisor Kenneth Hahn replied, "This isn't a demonstration. It is a prayer."

Then the seven of us knelt and sang "Singing for Our Lives." One by one, we were placed under arrest and taken away to jail.

Arrest for civil disobedience centered in a moral cause is an ever new challenge for Christians. Many ask, "What can I do? Problems seem insurmountable." I thought about this during my eleven-hour incarceration in jail, including four hours when I was chained to a bench while also handcuffed to another prisoner. The hours grew longer and longer, approaching midnight. I felt pain and discouragement.

I meditated. I prayed. I acknowledged my total absence of any control. I asked for help because I felt helpless. And, I received help. A tremendous peace, a centering, a trust, and an awareness that I was secure in God's control, took over my life. I realized: Jesus doesn't give up, so we can't give up either. Problems are not insurmountable, but solvable. Instead of being overwhelmed, we can take a leaf from A.A.—and approach "The Big Picture" a step at a time. And, believe. And, work at it. And, giving up the illusion of control, ask God to enable us to serve the cause of peace and justice in the world.

As lesbians and gay men explore new forms of theology and spirituality growing out of our consciousness and experience, we will discover fresh truths about ourselves and our tasks in the world.

One task is to heal and nurture others, including the church wherever it has become a dysfunctional spiritual family; where hate is found in it instead of love; when it stands in the way of justice instead of being an active instrument of wholeness; and where any part of the church has become monarchial, rigid, xenophobic, arrogant, unyielding to the Holy Spirit—and forgotten humility and servanthood, rooted in the humility and self-emptying servanthood of Jesus Christ.

I find at least three specific areas where our healing and nurturing gifts, as Christian lesbians and gay men, are presently needed.

1. *We need to help closeted gay people who suffer because they do not yet understand the Good News was meant for them, too.* Until they validate its joy within themselves, they cannot proclaim the Good News of their liberation in Jesus Christ—and come out like Lazarus from a dark tomb— saying, "Thank God for who I am!"

2. *We need to help men and women who are homophobic and oppose our civil and human rights.* In their Christian fundamentalism, the law takes precedence over grace. This is heresy, and millions have suffered because of it. In the flat, linear literalism that becomes their focus of life, the epiphany of God's continuing revelation is aborted. These men and women who want to see us silenced, imprisoned, or dead, stand in the way of Christ's love. Christ calls us to such a deep level of conversion that we may willingly offer them unconditional love. As nonviolence is Jesus Christ's response to violence, so it must be ours. Our mission is to change hearts and minds, by means of Christ's love, and create a new society.

3. *And, we are needed by Christ to help people who wonder: "How can we relate the sexual and the spiritual in our lives?* Is the nuclear family the only channel available for sexual expression that finds favor with God? Is love itself rigidly codified, and sex so hemmed in by barbed wire that it is a cause of judgment, guilt and spiritual failure?"

Our witness is to thank God for the union of the sexual and the spiritual that we have experienced in our own lives. Our witness is to the extended family where we deeply experience the joys and meanings of marriage in lesbian and gay unions. Our witness is to affirm sexuality as we believe Jesus Christ experienced it—Jesus Christ, a human being and therefore inescapably a sexual being, in the teaching of the incarnation which is a cornerstone of the church's faith.

We are a deeply moral people. We have persevered against the most outrageous calumny. God has a purpose for us. We are a blessed people with a mission, and we are called to love and joy.

Malcolm Boyd celebrated in 1990 the thirty-fifth anniversary of his ordination as an Episcopal priest. At the same time, the twenty-fifth anniversary edition of his classic book of contemporary prayers, Are You Running With Me, Jesus?, *was published.*

He is Chaplain of the AIDS Ministry Commission of the Episcopal Diocese of Los Angeles. He served from its inception on the AIDS Task Force of the City/County of Los Angeles. Author of 23 books, including Gay Priest *and* Look Back in Joy, *he's been a fellow at Yale; a civil rights, peace and AIDS activist; a parish priest and college chaplain; a Holly-wood TV producer; a playwright, magazine columnist and film critic.*

Malcolm Boyd lives in Los Angeles with his life-partner, Mark Thompson.

Nancy L. Wilson
Soul and Body

When, at age twenty-one, I walked into my first gay bar ("The 1270" on Boylston Street in Boston), it was like walking through the looking glass for the first time to the right side. The music playing on the juke box that night is burned forever in my memory. I knew the sheer joy of seeing women dancing with women and men with men, understanding for the first time why anyone would want to dance with anyone. This engaged my every nerve, all of my body. For the first time, I felt fully alive and embodied in a public place. I remember how I trembled, holding and dancing publicly with a woman whom I had only previously held that close in bed. A wall between our private and public life came crashing happily down around us.

That same month, I walked into my first Metropolitan Community Church service, in the little chapel at the Arlington Street Church (Unitarian) also on Boylston Street. Sitting with eleven or twelve other gay and lesbian people, I wept through communion. Body and soul were united on Boylston Street in my twenty-first year when I simply walked through the looking glass to my new spiritual home. I felt naked and vulnerable in the presence of a God who was not ashamed to be called my God. I found out that embodied freedom was possible for me, a lesbian Christian.

I am grateful to the core of my being, to being born a lesbian in the latter half of the twentieth century, and that when I came out a fledgling gay church was there to greet me. I can only imagine what it would have been like to be a lesbian with a call to Christian ministry at any other time in history.

Growing up lesbian in the fifties and sixties was a lot like being on the wrong side of the looking glass. For me, it was a bizarre blending of "'Alice in Wonderland' meets Paul's lament in I Corinthians 13, 'Now we see through a mirror dimly....'" I suppose I am unrepentantly a gay/lesbian "essentialist," believing that my lesbianism is as old as I am, with the quality of givenness, an ontological quality not unlike (though not identical to) ethnicity.

That essentialist bias is qualified by my understanding that human sexuality is a complex matrix of factors. Like many gay philosophers and poets, I believe that gay men and lesbians are a curious amalgam of "ethni." So I do not believe our gay culture is solely the creation of external, sociological, oppressive forces. At the core we experience a deep longing for our "kind." Through a world-wide homophobic fog we are beginning to see, even dimly, the outlines of a global gay and lesbian reality. It is diverse and peculiar in every culture, yet united at some deep, mysterious core of being. We are everywhere.

But, oh, the cost of knowing that. Ours is the generation of transition, layers and layers coming out, clearing the fog. We know now the joy of seeing each other, while we try to heal the pain of all the years of not seeing.

In the midst of this, some of us ask: Who is God in our struggle and celebration? Jesus of Nazareth, Cosmic Christ, what have you to do with us? How can we incarnate you in our body and blood?

We are sexual outlaws like those Christ ate and drank with. Ones who break the rules about gender and roles, the trans-people, whose very existence exposes the lies of patriarchal ontology. We are very dangerous.

I think it was Reverend Jim Sandmire who first pointed out that it was at Metropolitan Community Church that gays and lesbians in the U.S first gathered in large groups openly in the daylight. That event, that moment in history, is only a little more than twenty years old. It's too close to us; we are too close to it. We can't yet understand the magnitude of this shift in consciousness.

My childhood was a sexual/spiritual riddle straining, begging to be solved. All the clues were there, but there was no one to help me interpret them. Though I knew I was loved by my parents, two younger brothers, and a large extended family, there was always some alienation. It took a long time to understand.

During my childhood, I battled with asthma. I was two children: a sickly, isolated child, and an apparently healthy, bright, and invincible one. I went to great lengths to hide or minimize my disability. Asthma, after all, was a "wimp's" disease, and my strong, young lesbian self was ashamed. My struggle to breathe, I now know, was deeply connected to my struggle for embodied freedom. I simply couldn't breathe in a heterosexist, sex-negative, misogynist, racist, disembodied environment. (Welcome to the fifties.) My lesbian, healthy self, not getting the positive attention she needed, could barely breathe.

But there were moments. I have a vivid memory of six-year-old Nancy standing on her bed, looking out the window to our back yard on a warm, summery Long Island morning. I jumped up and down on my bed, naked at least from the waist up. Jumping and dancing, I was in the process of getting dressed when I was interrupted by the view outside the window. As I jumped ecstatically, looking out, I ran my hands up and down my torso. I felt my chest and rib cage, touching my little girl's body. Was I laying hands on my chest in an unconscious gesture of self healing? Or, just enjoying the touch of my hands on my skin? I was not alone; God and I were not separate in that moment of simple ecstasy. Loved, healthy for the moment, I was free and jumping for joy in my own private epiphany.

I still occasionally jump for joy when I hold my lover, Paula, in my arms, or preach, or walk, or serve communion, or laugh and weep with a dying friend, or play the piano. Voices inside still urge me to control, hide, and suppress my jumping for joy. It's too dangerous. No one should love being alive this much, love embodied freedom this much.

The year was 1962. Miss Mackin, my fifth grade teacher, was the most beautiful woman I'd ever seen. Irish and witty, she blushed easily. Unmarried and a devout Catholic, she adored Jack Kennedy. Since my father was from Massachusetts, I seized the opportunity to imitate a Boston accent in front of the class for Miss Mackin's benefit. She loved it. I was in heaven.

I remember when my friend Barry Levy confessed in front of the class that he had a crush on Miss Mackin. He said he routinely rode his bike in front of her house. I recall the intense mixture of pleasure and shame I felt in knowing that I did the same thing. But I didn't dare confess. In fact, for fear of running into Barry, I never rode past Miss Mackin's house again. Yet I'm sure that I thought about it every day for years.

Miss Mackin picked me to play Abraham Lincoln in our class play about the Civil War. It was the story of Lincoln's pardoning a soldier who fell asleep on duty. Our own Johnnie "Cry-baby" Gertz was typecast as the snivelling soldier. It is so obvious now that Johnnie was abused, physically and verbally. Was he targeted for abuse because he was gay? His life at school (probably at home too) was a daily emotional hell, a cycle of acting out punishment and tears. In our class play, he was the one pardoned, but he was never the one who needed to be forgiven.

Playing the part of Abraham Lincoln was the moral equivalent for me of being chosen prom queen. Tall and skinny, I was perfect for the part. I knew the Gettysburg Address by heart. I had read every book on Lincoln, including the obscure but informative *Abe Lincoln's Other Mother*, at the Fern Place

School Library. Those were days of innocent historical revisionism: Lincoln was the freer of slaves. I was *made* for this role! Tragic, dark, moody, the Great Emancipator was my hero, our veritable Christ of American history. Bless Margaret Mackin for overlooking the small detail that I was a girl. For just that moment, being female was not punishable and limiting. She understood me.

I threw myself into the role with abandon. I borrowed my cousin Billy's good Sunday suit, made my own hat and beard, and tried on my costume every day for weeks. I used my mother's eyebrow pencil to make my cheeks hollow and dark, my eyebrows thick and masculine.

Gayle, my very best friend all through elementary school, was miserable and pouting because she did not have a part in the play. We were unselfconsciously intensely bonded as a couple. I was "role-rehearsing" being in a lesbian relationship; I'm not sure what she was doing. In our daily after-school play we role-played Roy Rogers and Dale Evans. Ever feminine, though athletic, she always wanted to be Dale. That meant the role of Roy was mine. Aw shucks, ma'am, I pretended every now and then to be weary of always playing Roy. Inside, I was jumping for joy as sweet, humble, brave, toe-in-dirt Roy. Gayle and I played Roy and Dale through many long, lazy childhood summers, and rode our horses into seemingly endless sunsets.

From all the role playing, I felt, well, married to Gayle. When she "left" me for boys in junior high school in her heterosexual adolescence, I was close to being clinically depressed for a year. Gayle knew and had loved me, I thought. Abandoned on rocky shores of puberty, I was devastated. Now I needed to turn my cowboy hat and holster in for hose and heels, and pretend to be a "real" girl. Was my life over? I didn't dare tell anyone.

Later, I wrote a part for Gayle in our school play. When I showed it to Miss Mackin, she agreed to add it to the script. Gayle was happy; my "marriage" seemed to be saved.

I was always rescuing Gayle. She didn't do well in school and may have been abused at home. We were also acting out a co-dependent relationship which seemed to be the only option!

Gayle was Mrs. Lincoln in the play. Her mother made her a floor-length green satin gown for the occasion. The class hummed "The Battle Hymn of the Republic" as I recited the Gettysburg Address. Gayle entered, sweeping onto the stage in Loretta Young fashion. She said, "Mr. Lincoln, would you like some tea?" "No, thank you, dear," came the reply from the Great Emancipator. That was it, our moment. I was her hero, her President, and knight in shining armor. She was my First Lady. For five whole minutes the world was a friendly, understandable place where I got to write the script, have the starring role and also the leading lady of my choice.

My mother was in the audience. A woman seated next to her said, "So, who's the little boy playing Abraham Lincoln?" Later, my mother admitted that she replied, "I don't know." I recall my feelings of shock and hurt as if I'd been snatched in mid-air, caught and convicted of the crime of jumping for joy. But I covered up my hurt by laughing off my mother's act of betrayal and pretended I didn't know why she would be afraid, confused and ashamed. While I had been so thrilled at my acting debut, my mother had to pretend she didn't know me. This was my first overt homophobic message. How could I have loved and enjoyed doing something that so embarrassed my mother?

"Miss Mackin," I wanted to say, "I'll love you until I die for picking me to play Lincoln. You knew I didn't want to be a boy. I just wanted to be free to do what they did, to dress like I wanted to dress. To love whom I wanted to love, and be someone special and important. To have it my way."

Later on in puberty, I would fantasize I had a long-lost twin brother. All my girlfriends admired and fell in love with him. He could do all the things I couldn't. He didn't entirely disappear from my fantasy life until I left home and came out. He was the safe repository for unacceptable feelings and ambitions.

The lesbian part of my childhood was like a silent movie. There were clues, and pictures, but no words were spoken. Silences were part of my heritage: my mother's Quaker roots, my grandfather's Native Canadian blood, my grandmother's way of being silent when angry. Silence about lesbianism was simply part of a complex pattern of silences in my life.

My grandparents lived on a farm in New Hampshire. Our yearly family treks there are among my sweetest childhood memories. I loved the physicality of the farm, the piney air and the smells in the barn. Silently, I accompanied my grandfather all morning as we did chores together. The barn was decorated with thirty years of New Hampshire license plates (for cars, trucks and tractors) all proclaiming the state motto "Live Free or Die." As that phrase shouted out from the barn, it echoed in my silence. Was this another clue in the riddle? I had to find a way to live freely.

My grandparents had two special friends, Frank and Ricci. These two men, one white, one black, had lived together a long time. They resided in what my grandparents euphemistically called an "artists' colony" in rural New Hampshire, and had a home filled with braided rugs, handmade placemats, and all kinds of crafts, houseplants and baked goods. They were my first fairies! They lived in an enchanted, wonderfully decorated house, and my grandparents loved them. Mary and Isabel, two telephone operators from New York who bought a farm in New Hampshire, were also friends of my grandparents. These became powerful messages of hope for me. I resolved to move to New Hampshire as soon as I was able to leave home. People in New Hampshire seemed to be able to live any way they wanted.

At age thirteen, several events coincided in my life. My grandfather, who had gay friends (though the words "gay" and "homosexual" were never spoken) and knew some secret of embodied freedom, died. Gayle left me, and feminine expectations encroached. Soon I had a deep, unrequited crush on my seventh grade music teacher. I have a clear memory of feeling afraid, sad, and utterly alone in an unfriendly world. Something seemed to be terribly wrong with me. I was an alien in my family, in my world.

One summer night, I cried out to a God I really didn't know. I prayed into a hot, humid, black, still night sky. A street light glowed, steady and intense. Suddenly, something came to me through the window. I couldn't escape it or see it. Irresistibly, it enveloped me. It spoke to me, finding a voice deep within me, and said clearly and firmly, "I am your Friend, and someday you will have other friends. But for right now, I'm all you need." The night and light bathed me in a moment of still wonder. I knew there wasn't anything wrong with me. God was the Voice, and God was my friend, and the promise of more friends of my own "kind" sustained me through the awkward, confusing silences of a lesbian adolescence. If God was indeed for me, who could be against me? Even if the world was not a friendly place, I could survive and even hope for happiness.

That night I broke through a spiritual silence. I still did not know or understand that I was a "lesbian." But I knew that my differentness was not only okay with God, but part of some inkling of a destiny for me. God would use my uniqueness if I had the courage to claim and embody my freedom.

The next year two things happened. I met Jean over the piano after Girls' Chorus, busily putting away music for the teacher we both had a crush on. In the process of competing for the teacher's approval and attention, Jean and I "recognized" each other. Here was another one. Another what, precisely, I had no idea. It would take another five or six years to find out.

During that time, we began a passionate, stormy, lesbian relationship, but without sex. When Jean's upwardly mobile family moved away from our working class neighborhood, Jean and I wrote daily letters, sneaked phone calls, contriving ways to meet in Manhattan, yet all the while unable to name the nature of our feelings. We argued theology, politics, wrote poetry, she wrote music, we exchanged volumes of letters. Trying to hide my feelings for Jean from my mother, I raced to the mailbox to get her letters before my mother saw them. I tried to act casual about calls or visits from Jean. And, I'm sure I failed.

When I was sixteen, Jean came to my house for an overnight visit. She slept in my bed, although we never really touched. All night I thought of nothing else but the nearness of this precious one, a woman like me, whom I longed to hold, and hold onto. She got up early in the morning and took the train. But she left a message in lipstick on my mirror, a big heart with the words "I love you" in the middle. When I saw the message, my heart jumped for joy, and then stopped in terror. Furiously, I took kleenex and erased that lovely message in mortal fear my mother would see this and...know. Know what? I couldn't even let myself comprehend what it was my mother would know. So, torn between my great pleasure in that sweet message, and my fear...and hating my cowardice, I erased, erased, erased the message. Erased the love I didn't believe I could have.

That same year, when I took my first trip by myself through Manhattan to Connecticut to see Jean, I had to take a cab from Penn Station to Grand Central Station. I'd never been in a cab before, so didn't know strangers didn't ride together in cabs. A man got in the cab with me and tried to attack me. At a stop light, I managed to jump out of the cab with my bags. Stunned and frightened, I made my way to Grand Central Station. There I found refuge, I thought, in an empty car on the train headed to Westport. But eight or nine men, smelling of alcohol, sat around me in the car. For some reason, the porter didn't rescue me or help me to another car. For the next two hours, these men verbally abused, teased and threatened me. I remember very little of what actually happened, but when I got off the train, Jean and her father were waiting for me.

For nearly fifteen years I never told anyone that story. At the time, I believed if I told anyone what had happened, my parents would never let me go by myself to visit Jean again. I couldn't risk losing her. Gradually, silence and shame enshrouded the memory; I came to associate the danger and abuse with my homosexual feelings. My erotic, passionate feelings (still submerged then) were dangerous. They made me a target of punishment. I felt that I had no recourse, no right to be outraged, or rescued, or avenged. Later, I would talk about my understanding of oppression: "If you're gay, you pay." You pay if you stay in the closet with paranoid fears, low self-esteem, a fragmented sense of self, a compromised integrity, a life of half-truths and habitual cover-up or other self-destructive addictions and behaviors, including risky sexual behavior. On the other hand, if you come out of the closet, you pay with ostracism: persecution (physical, psychological, spiritual, social), and the potential loss of family, friends, job and community. I always knew I preferred to pay the price of coming out.

The second thing that happened after meeting Jean in 1964 was that I came to understand God was calling me to the ministry. I discovered the Bible and theology, read sermons and excelled in Sunday School. One day, I just knew. Coming home from church, believing my family would feel proud and supportive, my announcement was greeted by stony silence. Eventually, my mother expressed disapproval and fears. She said I was too sensitive, too "intense." What would my husband think? Didn't I really want to be a music teacher? My father took me to see the senior pastor, who informed us that theological education was wasted on women, since they just get married anyway. I knew my dad felt bad for me. He and I argued a lot about politics and religion that year, and in years to come. I knew he loved and respected me, yet he didn't understand who I was, either.

But then, a very wonderful event happened. As a fourteen-year-old girl, I knelt beside the gentle assistant pastor of the Methodist Church I attended and concelebrated communion during an early morning mid-week Lenten service. When I told him of my call to the ministry, he miraculously believed me and invited me to lead the Lenten services with him. Reading the liturgy, touching the bread and juice, was intoxicating. I jumped for joy. I knew that ministry was my destiny.

I came out sexually as a lesbian on Holy Thursday in 1972 at the age of twenty-one. Two months earlier, I broke my silence, when I looked in a mirror and said, "You are a lesbian." I had never had sex with anyone, touched my own genitals or really taken a deep breath. I was a sexual "anorexic," starving for touch, imprisoned by a fear that if I let myself know I was a lesbian (realizing that the world was so unfriendly), I would lose the little love and acceptance I thought I had.

Finally, in a leap of ecstatic courage, I told a woman who was a dear friend that I was in love with her. The surprise and delight of making love to her that night still fills me. What was supposed to be queer, perverted and debased was, I found, lovely, sacred and healing. Even in our virgin awkwardness, I felt alive and radiantly welcomed into another's arms, mouth and body. Our lovemaking was the ultimate hospitality. That spring became a blur of sexual passion, exposed homophobic terror, college graduation, coming out to my parents: all the initial costs of embodied freedom.

I remember a warm autumn evening in the chapel on Boylston Street at the new Metropolitan Community Church of Boston. During communion the congregation began to sing softly, "Jesus loves me this I know, for the Bible tells me so." I felt my spirit yielding, melting into the arms of a God whose simple assurances flooded that moment. I tried to fight the sweet pleasure of giving in. Always I had believed that I must shield myself, and those close to me, from my passionate love of God, my longing for my own people, and my own sexuality and need to be touched. Now I was healed of that belief in the company of these new friends God gave me.

My first two years of Metropolitan Community Church ministry resembled a roller coaster ride. That fall, my picture appeared on the front page of the City section of the *Boston Globe*. I didn't "come out," I fell out. Immediately, the Boston University School of Theology was scandalized by my presence. Only Dr. Robert Treese's advocacy and friendship, coupled with the fact that I quickly cast my lot with Metropolitan Community Church and closed the door on the Methodist ministry forever, saved me from being expelled.

Feminist scholars and students in the Boston Theological Institute, many of whom were lesbians, ran from me as if I had the plague. Only securely heterosexual feminists seemed able to speak to me. Women I used to smile at, or dance with, at the "Saints" (a lesbian bar in Boston), snubbed me at school. While feminists were in the process of post-Christianizing themselves, I fell in love with the first church I felt included all of me. I became determined to integrate the best of feminist analysis and prophecy into our new movement. I came to believe that Jesus Christ was in the midst of the embodied freedom I was embracing, just as other feminists were running from the least hint of traditional Christology.

I found myself to be a religious and sexual outlaw in the early seventies. This was replete with irony for me because I was a descendant of many religious and political outlaws. On my mother's side, I am a descendant of Elder William Brewster, "Chaplain" aboard the Mayflower, and Elias Hicks, a friend of Walt Whitman and founder of the radical "Hicksite" Quakers. I am an heir of the Brewsters and Princes of Scrooby, not far from Nottingham and Sherwood Forest in England. I'm sure I am flesh and blood of the legendary Robin Hood and his "merry men!" On my father's side, I am a descendant of Native North American healers and hunters, and poor Scottish refugees who came to America. Quakers, Calvinists, Puritans, Indians and outlaws: the struggle for embodied freedom is ancient in me.

In the early seventies, I was just moving into feminism. But I could not identify with middle-class feminists, and they shrank from the working-class and street-culture roots marking the early gay movement in America.

During my early ministry as a lesbian spiritual leader of a gay and lesbian congregation, there were many crises. I had to disarm several people who aimed guns and knives at me in church. Once, while I was celebrating communion, a man raced up to the altar, knocked over the sacred elements and punched me in the face. We had frequent bomb threats. One night, a group of fundamentalists came into our worship. During the Lord's Prayer they began to shout obscenities. We gathered in a circle, singing, until they departed.

There were astounding miracles. One Thanksgiving Day, two elderly women, one black, one white, knelt at the altar for communion. They had been together for forty years since meeting in a bar owned by Marlene Dietrich in Berlin. They came to the U.S. where Eva, who was German, was deported for nine years during World War II. Afterward, she returned to the U.S., and they lived in conservative Woburn, Massachusetts as "Mrs. Winne and her maid, Connie."

Now Connie was in her seventies and Eva in her eighties. They knelt together as the lovers and equals they were for the first time openly at the altar of MCC in Boston. It was my privilege to serve them the eucharist that day. They regaled me for many years with incredible tales of gay life in the first half of the twentieth century. Eva had been the lover of a baroness prior to World War I and had gambled her money away at Monte Carlo. Eva told me privately that she was an atheist, but took communion to please Connie. She spoke ominously of the re-emergence of fascism that she perceived in the U.S. in the mid-seventies.

In those days, I watched gay teenagers die of alcoholism by the dozens. And, I saw children and young gay people beaten senseless by police in bars and at police stations. I went to court again and again to help them. Suicides took an endless variety of forms. A deacon at Metropolitan Community Church in Providence, whose Catholic guilt and father's rejection drove him berserk, handcuffed himself to a chainlink fence, doused himself with gasoline and immolated himself. If I am ever tempted to see an idyllic time of gay and lesbian carefreeness before the AIDS epidemic, I stand corrected. There may have been moments of "Camelot" in a few gay centers in the U.S., but embodied freedom has clearly never come easily.

The first woman clergyperson that I ever saw wearing a clerical collar was myself in a mirror. We had no time for formalities. Just one month in seminary, I was the most theologically educated MCC women clergy-in-the-making. Larry Bernier, the founder of MCC in Boston, just dressed me in a collar and I began preaching, serving communion and pastoring. Three years later, I was ordained in Metropolitan Community Church after I had pastored two churches. I remember working very hard to make myself look older than my twenty-two years. MCC had about twenty churches then. It was a very young, fly-by-night operation, and I simply had no idea how important the vision of MCC, and of a gay and lesbian spiritual re-awakening, would become.

In MCC, I cut my ecumenical teeth. Suddenly, I found myself in the company of Pentecostals, Evangelicals, Catholics and Salvationists, whose vocabularies of faith and worship were strange, attractive and sometimes alienating. Meanwhile, we just did the best we could, expressing our need of one another and mutual love. We sacrificed precious dogmas and precious practices just in order to be together. I hated wearing a clerical collar. I found it a "slave" symbol that had ironically come to mean male spiritual superiority and privilege. This was politically and theologically repulsive to me. But I wore it (although I rebelled and didn't wear one at my ordination), because it shocked the world to see a woman in one. It might have been pure transvestism to me, like wearing my cousin Billy's suit to play Abe Lincoln. A lavender clerical shirt, blue jeans and a lavender blue jeans jacket was the favorite outfit of my early ministry.

I remember meeting Troy Perry, the founder of MCC, when he came from Los Angeles to preach at MCC in Boston. Just one week before our first encounter, the Los Angeles MCC church had been burned to the ground by arsonists. I was impressed that he left his church in crisis to visit us. I was predisposed not to like Troy. He was a white, southern male. Someone had said he looked a bit like Elvis Presley. I was prepared to be turned off, defensive and skeptical. But as I entered the little ante room at Arlington Street Church, he jumped up to greet me. Encountering an overpowering presence, I jumped back, afraid to trust. When he preached, however, I heard a radical message of justice, unhindered grace, and irresistible humor, in an enthusiastic Pentecostal style. It won me instantly. He was prophetic, charismatic and gay, and my heart leapt in joy. Suddenly, I realized that our new community comprised of liberals, feminists, Catholics, Evangelicals, Pentecostals, outlaws, a few communists, prostitutes, street kids, Republican bankers, refugees from prisons and mental hospitals, college professors, and truck drivers, could make church together.

That was seventeen years ago. Since that time, my life has been given to ministry in MCC. I've spoken at the White House, to the Governing Board of the National Council of Churches, before "governors and kings." But my greatest joy has been pastoring an MCC church on a daily basis. I have the privilege of participating in the healing and empowering of my own people, the friends whom God promised me. Today, I still see Christ crucified in the wounds, both external and self-inflicted, festering in our people. A whole generation of gay and lesbian youth growing up in the midst of the AIDS holocaust needs to claim embodied freedom in fresh, challenging new ways.

Jesus Christ, enflesher of God, has come to me in the process of embracing my lesbianism and my spiritual embodied freedom as a child of God. Jesus is enfleshed in our life and death struggle with AIDS. The Word is shouting through the silences of centuries: Gay and lesbian children of the Most High God, Live in freedom!

Nancy L. Wilson is a native of Plainview, New York, and a graduate of Allegheny College. She attended Boston University on a Rockefeller Scholarship and received a Masters of Divinity from SS. Cyril and Methodist Seminary (Roman Catholic) in Orchard Lake, Michigan.

She has served Metropolitan Community Churches in Boston, Worcester, and Detroit. She was re-elected to the Board of Elders of the Universal Fellowship of Metropolitan Community Churches for a fourth term in 1987.

Since 1986, Nancy has been the Senior Pastor of Metropolitan Community Church of Los Angeles, the denomination's Founding Church. Nancy has also been the chief spokesperson for UFMCC's ongoing dialogue with the National Council of Churches of Christ in the USA. She resides with her lover of thirteen years, Paula Schoenwether, in Los Angeles.

SANDRA ROBINSON
Census of the Soul

As Black women, as lesbians and feminists, there is no guarantee that our lives will ever be looked at with the kind of respect given to certain people from other races, sexes or classes. There is similarly no guarantee that we or our movement will survive long enough to become safely historical. We must document ourselves now.[1]

*I*n my alone times, when I was a child, I wondered who I was before I was and I saw stars and dark. I tried to imagine what I was when I was not and I felt comfort. I wished sometimes to be there again. I dreamed and longed for the warm dark arms that rocked me and protected me. Someone, somehow told me that this feeling was not real, but I talked to my invisible friend anyway. We played together, we cried together and we wished for mother together. I promised my friend that I would never forget our wonderful times together—stolen afternoons in the attic reading my treasure trove of old comics and my first real book, *Little Journeys Into Storyland,* the only book I would have for many years that was written by "Negroes" and to the unending astonishment of my child's mind—for "Negro" children like me. Despite my suspicions that I must surely be losing my mind, I talked openly and innocently aloud to my friend as I channeled my budding artistic abilities on the 100-year-old wedding portrait of my great-great grandparents (an heirloom carelessly left to atrophy in the desperately dusty gloom of the attic) or combing my Teddy's fur with hair pomade. During these times, I assured my friend that I would never forget. I was afraid that in growing up, I would lose my friend.

I went to church and church said that there was God. "God," church said, "was an old white man in the sky with a long white beard who sat on a throne." My friend and I were confused. "White" was probably never stated, rather implied, but the mystery was only complicated when at the tender age of eight I saw the 1936 film "The Green Pastures," the all-"Negro" production of Marc Connelly's fable of life in heaven. "De Lawd" was played by Rex Ingram, a dark black man who bore little resemblance to any characterizations of God in any of the Sunday School books. In science class, school said that there was earth with atmosphere around it called sky and beyond that was dark, vacuum and stars and planets and suns. Where then, was heaven? My friend and I were confused. School said that the universe was unlimited and there was no end to time and space—my friend and I remembered romping there before I was. But church said there was a heaven in a place like a city where only good people went—where choirs sing, angels fly and people praise God all the time and no one ever did anything wrong. My friend and I thought that that was boring.

I never told anyone about my friend until now. If it had not been for my friend in my beginning times, I could not have lived well because life and people were not always fun then and they could not have understood how hard it was. My friend told me that I was OK and held me when I became angry and afraid and I could not show it to people. When my parents were not with me, my friend protected my softness from my grandmother's hardness. My friend had many names, and sometimes we spent hours trying to find the right name.

As I grew, I began to see parts of my friend in my great-grandmother— when she told stories about the times before the banality of the present—the exciting times when Duke Ellington and Cab Calloway were just beginning their careers and stayed in people's homes because the hotels were "whites only," the times when they stayed in our neighborhood and ate her food. It would be at these times, these rare times, that my grandmother would suddenly seem actually happy, remembering her close friend, Ivy—one of the Duke's first singers—beautiful Ivy, who gave my grandmother a pair of red shoes. I would hear that story told exactly the same way, never an expression left out or diminished, until I left home at twenty-two years old. My grandmother's deepest love was this woman who lived on the road at intersections of untold adventures—my grandmother, conservative, practical, righteous to a fault, who carefully taught me to never become too close to other women. My friend and I saw behind the stories and felt between the words, images of song and dance about pain, pain tempered and controlled by an unnamed sensual meaning, pain played like an instrument to timeless rhythms by people who carefully crafted their pride, people who knew the answers as well as the questions but had no need to expound upon them. My grandmother's fear of losing herself to this unnamed sensuality would not let her give into it. But my great-grandmother was not afraid and was made whole by her courage.

I saw parts of my friend in my godmother. She held me and loved me and believed I was wonderful. She loved beautiful things and collected delicate porcelain miniatures of women and candy dishes (which, to my delight, were kept full). She was a beautiful woman—sweet, giving, modest and self-effacing. When we went to visit, she spent most of our time together on the phone. I was an adult before I realized that this was how she survived. She was married to an alcoholic who beat her on a regular basis. He had been wounded in the war (or so the story goes), and was on disability. His paycheck went to pay for his habit and my godmother was left to her own devices to pay for their home and buy food on the money she made running numbers. She was humble and never criticized her husband. She took the beatings quietly, often lost bill money to him when he would find her hiding places and staunchly refused to leave him when her friends begged her to go, saying, "He needs me." Sometimes I would tell her how hard it was living with my grandmother, and I could feel her understanding. She taught me how to endure, how to protect my most important parts so that I would not be devastated. She taught me about strength and beauty. One day Richard broke up all of the pretty things she collected, and not long after that Ella Lee died quietly of a deadly tumor in her stomach.

And then there was Becky. We were fascinated by Becky. Becky was the local carpenter. She was a tall woman, built like a tree, strong and stable. Becky wore men's clothes, drove the oldest car I had ever seen, wore her hair short and looked like an Apache. I would do anything to be near Becky, to watch her as she worked. I would stare longingly at her, not even knowing why she fascinated me so. My grandmother did everything in her power to keep me away from Becky. It occurs to me now that I stared at Becky in much the same way that I find children staring at me when I am shopping or in any places where there are children. My friend and I had many conversations about Becky. Everyone in the neighborhood liked her and they appreciated her work, but she was clearly regarded as different and never invited into any social gatherings, even though she lived just around the corner from us. Ironically, it was my homophobic grandmother who helped me to understand about Becky and opened a path of understanding why I was so intrigued. My grandmother must have sensed something in me that prompted her to tell me stories about her roommate at Wilberforce College, who supposedly made sexual advances toward her against her will. My grandmother carefully explained to me what a bulldyke is and cautioned me that these people are to be avoided because of the "terrible" hold that they have on other women. She did not bother to discuss the "sinful" nature of women like them, rather she believed that scare tactics would work as well. I remained irreversibly intrigued and desperate to find out more about the secrets of these wondrously powerful women. They must have been powerful for my grandmother to be so afraid of them.

As I grew into young womanhood, I betrayed my fantasy friend and tried to substitute what church said for the friend of my childhood. I discovered quickly that I was not comforted or protected by the old man in the sky. One evening after Baptist Training Union, I went downstairs in the church to get something that I had forgotten. A deacon, known for his active interest in young women, followed me and attempted to force himself on me. I threatened to tell the church about him and he left me alone. I was nineteen years old, and that was the last time I attended a Baptist church activity.

Youngstown, Ohio was a steel town and the seventh largest city in Ohio. The home of Youngstown State University was a mixed bag of Polish, Irish, Italian and black ethnicity. Economically, it was predominately blue collar during my formative years.

The community I grew up in was middle class, black Baptist, and African and Christian Methodist Episcopal churched. Social status was determined by membership in fraternal and sorority activities and community service organizations. I pledged Delta Sigma Theta and Gamma Sigma Sigma Service Sorority. My grandfather and my father were both Masons. My great-grandmother was a precinct committee woman for the Republican Party and had been the president of the Ladies Aid Society for forty years before finally retiring. During my teens and college years, President Johnson's poverty program was flourishing, and it was a plus to be liberal and a Democrat. Older affluent blacks were grudgingly giving up their allegiance to the Republican Party, including my family, and keeping a doubtful eye on Martin Luther King, Jr. (My great-grandmother kept up the tradition of loyalty to the Republican Party because Lincoln freed the slaves and Lincoln was a Republican. She went to her grave believing that the Republicans would again come through.) Younger blacks were swept up in the vogue of black militancy and afros.

Leaving the church was more than an act of rage. It was also a mixed act of survival and rebellion. It would be years before I would be able to understand how important communal worship was to oppressed American blacks because of my feelings of being at odds with, or different from, my people. I knew that I was different, but at that time I had no way of knowing why or how I was different.

I experienced my first "coming out" at sixteen. It was my debut. My grandmother was absolutely determined to officially introduce me to society in an elegantly staged event at a local park that was often rented out for such occasions as this. I was terrified. I had not felt such intense anxiety since performing to "I'm a Little Teapot" on television when I was eight years old. In tutu and ballet shoes, I mechanically moved through the repeatedly rehearsed steps to the tinny-sounding refrain of a piano, still desperately trying to imitate a teapot for one of many humiliating recitals—this one not confined to proud and preening parents, rather to the small red light on the camera that, I was told, represented the whole viewing public of Youngstown, Ohio. My coming out party, I was convinced, was a disaster. Most of the people who came were my grandparent's friends. It seemed an eternity before my school friends arrived. All of us were uncomfortable trying to go through the expected motions of newly aged ladies and gentlemen. My grandmother stayed angry with me throughout the evening because I was so stiff and did not become the kind of charming girl that would attract her ideal of the perfect boyfriend. I thought that I had made a gallant effort. I secured a boyfriend soon after that to calm her concerns and unknowingly began the ritual of young dykeletes-to-be of keeping the treasured secrets of unrequited love of women.

They told us in school that it was natural to have some feelings beyond friendship in our same-sex friendships, but that we would grow out of it. I waited patiently to grow out of it—to make the rite of passage past this stage. Ten years, two engagements to men and two lesbian relationships later, I still had not grown out of it. Unknown to me at the time, I was already well on the way to my second "coming out." It happened, as they say, one night at a gay nightclub. I had just moved from my home town. My employer, a black ex-marine, had heard rumors that I was a lesbian. When he threatened to fire me unless I slept with him to prove that I was not a lesbian, I knew that it was time to leave. In Columbus, Ohio I discovered, much to my amazement, that there were many other people like me. I was nearly twenty-nine years old before I realized that I was not growing out of it. A friend of mine took me to a popular gay disco near downtown. Sock hops, mixed couple after-hours socials, Greek parties, parties at black "country clubs"—none of these even remotely compared to the mystic and passionate energy of gay disco. This was my experience, and it was here that I found a right-ness, a natural-ness that I had not experienced in any other social setting. Dancing had always been a painful experience for me, more because of the mating rituals than knowing the right dance steps and movements. When I danced that night, it was with ease and gratitude. In the dance I reeled and whirled, watching the slick head of hair pulled back into a ball revealing the classic African profile of my female dance partner against the strobe-lit night. Six rum-on-the-rocks later, the effects of strobe lights, and the deafening bass run of the disco music mixed with extreme new emotions, took its toll on me.

The nausea came swiftly. In minutes, they helped me through the crowd and out into the merciful air-giving night and held me as I lost a fine Chinese meal against the tire of my Cutlass. Between heaves, my mind raced back and forth as a dying person seeing her total life rerun. My junior high peers had nicknamed me "professor." I was a Y-Teen, future teacher and loved sock hops. I was in the senior play and a member of the Latin Club. I survived the mysterious ostracism of the all-but-me white Junior Achievement Company that made a $200 profit from our metal potholders. I had two boyfriends who fought and almost died in Vietnam. Had I not been so sick at that moment, I would have chuckled in wonder at how I came to be here, losing my food in the parking lot of a gay disco, escorted by three women I hardly knew. Even now, fighting the death wish that accompanies nausea, I knew that I loved the adventure of it. I remembered Ralph Ellison's *Invisible Man* and the character's thoughts as he freed himself from the chaos around him:

> *The hibernation is over. I must shake off the old skin and come up for breath....I'm coming out, no less invisible without it, but coming out nonetheless.*

It was impossible for me to follow the traditions. In that world, I was a voice talking to walls, a communal drone inhibited by my femaleness and queer because of my odd aversion to housewifery and unwillingness to be the power "behind" any man. Suddenly, I was happy to be free of the responsibility to be dully the same as anyone. I felt a deeper responsibility to grow and, most importantly, to live.

A year later, in a more sedate setting, I joined my two closest friends for lunch. In college we were inseparable. One of them would be dead in six months from childbirth. These women, neither of them lesbians, "took me off the front porch" during my college years. They helped me develop some mother wit and recognized my lesbianism before I had the slightest clue. They stood by me and nurtured me. We laughed, comparing the folly of our old dreams with the realities of the present. I told them about my first experience in a lesbian bar, which was frequented by "untouchables" or, as some would say, "stone" women. They were butch women who patterned their relationships after heterosexual models and marriages. They could have been the bulldykes that my grandmother used to caution me about in horror-stricken terms. I remembered lines from an old song that my grandmother and her friends probably sang in playful earthy ridicule:

> *When you see two women walking hand in hand,*
> *Just look 'im over and try to understand,*
> *They'll go to those parties have the lights down low,*
> *Only those parties where women can go,*

You think I'm lying—just ask Tack Ann,
Took many a broad from many a man...

My grandmother had been so wrong. It was, in fact, the acting out of negative heterosexual role models of relationship and socializing that was their tragedy—not the fact of their sexual orientation. Unfortunately, negative models were all they had to imitate. They equated the natural loving emotions of being lesbian with evil and chose what was unnatural for them—heterosexual models—and used them as devices of punishment for themselves and their "wives," whom they oppressed in the same way that men oppress women.

We exchanged a few more memories and talked a bit about our plans for the future. Then they persuaded me to go back to my home town once more for good closure this time. I went. I visited the Baptist church where my family still worshipped. It had been eleven years since the incident with the deacon.

Miss Jane had false teeth. Of the changes I saw, her new teeth was the most unexpected. The women still wore grand hats and gloves to Sunday worship, which detracted from the natural beauty of their faces that maintained a fight to emerge from layers of pressed powder and lipstick. Rarely was their blue-dyed hair visible, fried into curls and parts that the most skilled beautician could not change after years of the same style. Estee Lauder still competed to steal the most breath from innocent bystanders. The bald-headed deacons in a land of afros resembled somber moustache-wearing undertakers. I noticed several Baptist priests-to-be walking about in their silent stupors, Bible under sweat-filled armpits, aspiring to celibate glory while inwardly battling the devil of unknown sexual ecstasy brought on by rapidly progressing puberty. Cobwebs were brushed away with regularity to keep up the impression of life and activity. The sterile corridors echoed the songs and voices of generations of Christians as the plastic paint in the building began to chip off in unnoticed places. Perhaps it was my poor vision, but the silent yellow of the walls seemed to take on a dull cast which stole the particles of sunlight that seep through stained glass windows—windows that characterize sixteenth-century white Europeans playing at their interpretations of holiness. I felt a surging sense of loss as I saw and talked with people whom I knew I would never see again and was reminded of our Matriarch—my beloved Gran (my great-grandmother), who loved me most. All of this in a fleeting rapture of race memory. She stayed with me, in me, during the communion. I was graced with her essence on this first Sunday morning. It was the time after the sermon of getting real. Here it was, the time when the community became one, the remembering of Christ's suffering and the acknowledgment of the amazing event of the missing body, the empty tomb. It was here that I learned that African-Americans did not just adopt Christianity because the plantation owners taught it to us, it was adopted because the experience of Christ is the experience of the oppressed and enslaved, the anamnesis, the experience of knowing, really knowing or being there! This was when the old saints would stamp their feet to a beat known only to their souls and hum/chant out the misery, sigh out the pain and know the miracle wrought by God that they survived to this moment. I felt the ancient dark arms wrap around me, and I knew a truth of God.

Even in knowing a truth communicated to us by others, we must rediscover it within the context of our own experience in order for it to apply to our own survival. I left Youngstown and went back to double life existence believing that I could find spiritual fulfillment without benefit of corporate worship and believing that I could grow whole living in the safety of my closet as I climbed a corporate ladder. I did climb successfully, not so much on my skill and expertise, but because I was a great token—not only was I black and female, but I was also very good at what I did in the insurance industry. I had escaped my family. My hateful grandmother's last words to me were that I would burn in hell if I kept living with women. I had made one last trip to visit her at Christmas time. I tried to be grown up, to make peace, but I made things worse. That night I stayed in the room where Gran (my great-grandmother) spent her last days. I had never been so desperately unhappy. My lover was spending Christmas with her family just ten miles away. This was a compromise of double life existence—if we pretended that we were not together, maybe no one would notice. This was a practice that we were both taught, the practice of keeping secrets. I felt Gran crying with me. I remembered how brutally my grandmother treated her before she died. She was very old at ninety-one. We didn't know anything then about Alzheimer's Disease, and when Gran could not remember things or even how and where to go to the bathroom, my grandmother scolded her and treated her like a disobedient child. I wept. I wept for Gran, I wept for my lover, I wept for myself. I knew that something had to change. Something inside me.

Only the black woman can say, "when and where I enter, in the quiet, undisputed dignity of my womanhood, without violence and without suing, or special patronage, then and there the whole...race enters with me."
Anna Julia Cooper, 1892

Four years later, some friends told me about a black woman coming to Columbus, Ohio to pastor the local Metropolitan Community Church. I didn't know very much about MCC, in fact I didn't really know anything about them, but I was certain that they were all white. In 1982 it was unheard of for a black to pastor an all-white or even predominately white congregation— and certainly not a woman, I thought. I did not believe that a church stating an outreach to the lesbian and gay community could be sincere, therefore I was not prepared for what I found.

Answering the demands of the Inner Voice (mine had been annoying me for the past four years to change something or go mad) always brings us face to face with the unknown and unexpected. It fills us with anxiety because it seems to encourage us to do the ridiculous. Not in my wildest dreams would I have guessed that this act of curiosity would lead me to seminary and ordination as clergy.

The worship was sincere and the sermon was packed with incredible statements that pronounced God's love for all people. Well, I had heard that one before but not about lesbians and gays. The preacher actually used the words "lesbian" and "gay" from the pulpit! Somehow I knew, without any doubt, that the things she said were true. I remembered, during the worship, the things I had done in my life. During communion, when we repeated a confession and paused for reflection, I realized that it had never been my sexual activity with women that I was guilty and ashamed of—it was my sexual relationships with men that I had always prayed for forgiveness. Without understanding it consciously, I knew, even then, that I had gone against my nature when I slept with men.

We must never presume, as I did, that because we have discovered or re-discovered life-changing truths about ourselves, that the world will auto-matically change with us or toward us.

In 1984, before attending my first Governing Board meeting of the National Council of Churches of Christ in the USA as an ecumenical officer of MCC, I called my former pastor. He came to pastor the Baptist Church in Youngstown when I was thirteen years old. For six years he had been an invaluable source of guidance and support for me through painful times with my grandmother. It was just weeks before I moved that I broke down and admitted to him that I had been sexually involved with a woman. Being a good counselor, he helped me process my feelings and did not condemn me. I called to tell him about my new position and to get support and encourage-ment from him to help me through my overwhelming fear at coming out in front of U.S. church leadership, many of whom were black clergy. Perhaps his reaction should have been predictable. I was surprised and deeply hurt when he became angry with me, demanding to know why it was necessary for me to announce to the world my sexual orientation. He told me that he knew many brothers in the clergy who were gay, but that they were properly married and no one knew. Why couldn't I follow their example and do more meaningful ministry? I pointed out the hypocrisy in his statements and reminded him that if we believe that God is real, God knows what we do in bed. I asked him if scripture anywhere guides us to keep secrets and live a lie. My questions went unanswered and we ended the conversation. I have not spoken to him since.

One day, on my way to work, I embraced a vision of change. Within that imagining, I felt my self removed from the seeming waste of corporate living. I had no money, my Datsun 280Z was history and my apartment walls were laced with books instead of fashionable prints. My execu-dyke clothes became worn jeans and plaid shirts. My work had something to do with people and the problems of living. I felt a cooling sentience nudging anxiety out of my being, and for a moment—just a moment—I felt an incredible, mysteriously undefinable joy.

The moment passed quickly, but I never forgot the feeling or the images. It was not asked for, prayed for, or otherwise summoned—it simply happened. It was the moment of liberating change. Its only need was to be recognized, reckoned with, consciously put somewhere in my memories for sustenance. Perhaps it was the ephemeral mind of God; perhaps it was, as some might say, need being the mother of invention; regardless, for me it was the focused moment of giving up what is unimportant for what is important, or more specifically, giving up illusions of well-being for what is really true. It was a reality that I could handle then, the entryway to land-scapes still hidden, which only come into view in the way that a room comes into view as one approaches it from a hallway and turns to walk through the doorway.

It was months later that I prayed for clarity in my struggle toward fulfillment. The time of asking, is it now that I risk coming out? Allowing God to be my raison d'etre? That prayer was answered, quickly, and suddenly the rooms of landscapes began to come into full view, one right after another, rollercoasting my being through time. And it was that moment of undefinable feeling that sustained me through years of heartbreaking growth; through the pains of naked humiliating fascism; through betrayals; through days with no money to pay bills, buy food or clothing; through dependency on fickle humanity for basic survival; through deaths of friends; through seemingly fruitless ministry; through the hypocrisy of the theologically insensitive.

Is it worth it? Of course. Within the experience of pain I discovered life that is worth living, people worth living for; and on a good day, just a hint of the power of God; and on bad days, when I am willing, I can sense God's chaotic nature, revealing dimly perceived regular patterns of bias toward good and, somehow, I know that even within the confusion and horror of life, it's the best adventure.

[1]J.R. Roberts, Black Lesbians: An Annotated Bibliography, Naiad Press, 1981, p.91.

Reverend Sandra Lynn Robinson is currently the Dean of Samaritan College, the professional school of the Universal Fellowship of Metropolitan Community Churches (UFMCC). UFMCC has a special outreach to the lesbian gay community. Dean Robinson completed her Master of Divinity degree at United Theological Seminary in Dayton, Ohio and was ordained in UFMCC in 1989. From 1984-1990, Robinson coordinated the dialogue between the UFMCC and the National Council of Churches of Christ in the USA and the World Council of Churches as director of the Department of Ecumenical Witness and Ministry for UFMCC. Robinson also directed the Department of People of Color in UFMCC from 1986-1989. She resides with Reverend La Paula Turner, her partner of eight years, in the San Gabriel Valley in southern California.

JONATHAN EMERSON

The Silent Muse
A Human Drama in Three Acts

Act I: Discovered

There I sat, fidgeting and trembling in the counselor's office. Not unlike the proverbial child caught with a grubby hand stuffed deep into the cookie jar. More like the only time from my childhood when I can remember being caught clowning around in class. To my delight I had discovered I could make the other kids laugh, but the teacher's rebuke cut deep, and shattered whatever notoriety I might enjoy. It seemed as though my whole raison d'être in life, even as a child, was to measure up to authority-figures. Even scoring a 99 on some test was only a hollow triumph, knowing that my father would ask why I had missed that one question.

It was my second year in a private Christian college. As for most nineteen-year-olds, the world's horizons seemed boundless. I was an adult; free of home, parents, and childish ways. I was meeting new people, making new friends, looking for that gusto in life I had heard so much about. As an only child, dorm life was probably the most fascinating, if not trying, facet of that existence. It was there, surrounded by men—in the halls, in their jockeys, and in the showers—where that still, small voice whispered the loudest: "You are different."

In high school I had dated my share of girls like anyone else. At least until the time to "make my move" was long past due and I would break it off.

College women seemed to like me. But their hands felt foreign in mine, and I could not seem to shake the images of all those preppy men, the jocks, the half-clad visions of maleness who paraded through the dorm. I much preferred *their* hands, *their* hugs; and we were, after all, an affectionate school. When, I wondered, would that part of me finally grow up?

Okay, so I was stuck, trapped in some pre-pubescent stage of life. Just give it time, I thought, one day you'll wake up and suddenly breasts will be of some interest. Besides, to whom could I confide this confusion? The Bible was clear, or so I had been taught, sex before marriage is wrong. Period. And sex with another man? That wasn't even sex. It was a perversion; an abomination; the unspeakable. The Bible had been my life since childhood, and now, in this Christian college, it began and infused every class, it was studied and discussed in every dorm, lives were made and broken by its content—that holy, inspired, and literal content.

About that time I began to keep a journal. It seemed the adult thing to do. I had fantasies about being a writer someday, and when I was finally famous, I reasoned, a journal would prove invaluable for future biographers. But even there, on those private pages, I could not bring myself to write a single word about the "flaw": that daunting obsession with the male of the species that would not be repressed despite my efforts.

The solution seemed simple enough. Keep two journals. Tucked neatly away in a locked drawer sat the real me; "A Diary of a Personal Problem," I had called it. How remarkable that I could not see the incredible psychic damage that second journal would inflict. Somehow, I believed that keeping that journal under lock and key would also keep that chunk of my life under wraps, safe and guarded from the light of day. Like lopping off my soul and hiding it away where it could do no harm.

So there I sat. I had been called into see the school's psychologist. The stage was set. He said we needed to discuss some problems with my roommate, which I reasoned was a good thing. He and I were not getting along.

"Frank believes you are headed for an emotional breakdown."

I was stunned. Sure, we were having problems, but a breakdown?

"Look," I began, trying to keep control, "this just hasn't worked out with Frank and me. I'd be more than willing to move out. I'm sure that would solve any..."

The counselor was not listening. He silently slid open a file drawer and produced a stack of photo-copied pages. As he handed them across the desk, I could not decide whether to vomit or burst into tears. There it was, "A Diary of Personal Problems."

At that moment any rational, secure human being would have taken the papers, threatened a lawsuit for invasion of privacy, and otherwise made a scene appropriate to the crime.

I sat there. Every drop of moisture had vanished from my mouth. The counselor began using the kind of soothing, condescending tones one might try on a cornered animal. I had visions of the whole school finding out how weird I was, what a vile, ugly sinner I had become. I had visions of telephone calls to Mom and Dad, of expulsion, of a life going down in flames. The counselor recommended a psychiatrist.

I spent the next week in a fog. Frank had moved out. The counselor had personally driven me to the local psychiatric hospital for an interview. Only later did I discover that they had reserved a room for me, "just in case." Maybe I was sick, I thought, maybe some chemical imbalance.

While escaping being institutionalized, I could not escape feeling sub-human. My desires were unnatural. Worst of all, they displeased God. My deepest feelings were in direct conflict with the way God had intended things to work. They might as well have told me I was possessed by the devil.

I burned my journal.

Act II: Out and About

Just two years later I found myself cradling a man in my arms while he wept. Philip was an old friend. We had gone to grade school, junior high, high school, and three years of college together. He had always been rather flamboyant, never very athletic and, I discovered, gay.

"I'm falling in love with Tom...I just can't help it," he said through the sobbing. "I thought I'd grow out of this...I'm sure Tom must be gay, don't you think? What if he isn't? Oh, I'll just kill myself if he isn't." Let us not forget the touch of melodrama.

I listened carefully. I sympathized with his plight. And all the while ready to cry like a baby myself. I could not very well let him cry alone. So I did it. I came out to Philip. This time without coercion, I came out. This time to whom and when I decided. This time for healing and for strength, and not humiliation. We talked nearly all night. We laughed. We cried. We screamed and ranted against God and the church.

"Who are they," we demanded to know, "to tell us what is natural? We didn't choose to be this way. And isn't it love that matters most to God anyway? Isn't that what the Bible is all about, love? How could God be angry with love?"

As true as that might be, very little love but a lot of sex followed that startling night. Our mutual revelation demanded some action, and we were ready to start living. Philip had a gay cousin who agreed to show us fledg-lings a night on the town. I will never forget my first gay bar. Feeling like a foreigner without a passport, I ventured in. The first thing I saw was a man greet another man with a kiss. On the lips! I never imagined it could be so easy, look so natural. It was exhilarating, not only to discover other men who felt as I did, but ones who actually acted on it. I was out. And I was home.

I soon discovered that "out" also meant "out late." We bar-hopped for hours, and when we finally emerged from our last stop on the gay circuit, the eastern sky was just beginning to lighten. Stumbling back to Philip's cousin's place, a one-bedroom, sparsely furnished flat, I soon realized all three of us would be crashing for a nap in that one queen-sized bed. Although exhausted, I was too intrigued by this to even close my eyes; Philip lying on one side, his cousin on the other.

Not daring to move (though yearning to do something in such an opportune situation), I got up to answer nature's call—the kind of call only quarts of beer can issue. While decided if flushing would disturb the others' sleep, I felt a hand on my shoulder. Philip's cousin (to this day I cannot remember his name, much to my chagrin) stood next to me, naked and obviously primed for an encounter.

The die-hard romantic in me had not envisioned my first sexual interlude in a bathroom. But who was I to argue? It was brief and to the point, but at least a fitting epilogue to our first night on the town.

Graduation came and went. I moved to the big city to be closer to where I imagined all the action was. I was not disappointed. I knew all the bars, thanks to a startling phenomenon called the gay press. I never even dreamed that a whole newspaper would be devoted to the concerns of gay men and lesbians. There is a whole community of us out there, I realized, and I hit every establishment I could manage (leather bars were still a bit beyond me). My first year in the city must have looked something like an American's first trip to Europe—if this is Tuesday this must be Paris.

Of course no one had really coached me on the fine art called "cruising." I did not even own anything resembling a traveler's dictionary of key phrases for the Tourist. Nevertheless, I learned quickly. While longing for love, I didn't really believe love was possible between two men, so I settled for the next best thing: lust. The dam had burst, apparently, the one that had, from years of repression, bottled up that driving desire for sexual contact.

I found myself in the oddest situations that year. Circumstances I never could have anticipated suddenly materialized, like sitting in my little two-seat sports car at three o'clock in the morning wishing I could get rid of that stick shift. Joe (an irrelevant choice of names since I cannot remember his either) was draped over the center console, arms wrapped around my neck, and, I discovered the next morning, giving me my first "hickey."

From there I graduated to a slightly larger car and to a city park in the dead of winter. The windows were heavily fogged. I was amazed that the man I had spotted earlier that night in the bar, the one I was certain would not even speak to me, the one with the incredible blond hair and equally astonishing green eyes, was now sprawled out in my back seat, pants wrapped around his ankles.

As the inevitable climax quickly approached (evidenced by his none-too-subtle rapid breathing), headlights cut through the clouded glass. Leaping in the driver's seat, I managed to flee the park before an embarrassing encounter with the local police. Trying to drive with belts, socks, and the loop of jockey shorts wrapped carelessly around the gas pedal is not recommended.

Sex was fun. And sex, not just genital activity, but sexuality, was liberating. Showing affection—a hug, a kiss, standing arm-in-arm with another man—broke that taboo-barrier our society so carefully creates, even demands, in our relationships. It is as if our culture expects intimacy, but only across a great chasm; physicality is not allowed. Our sexuality, I was pleased to learn, is a vital way in which we human beings communicate. It is, in fact, the bridge needed to cross that gulf. To affirm the goodness of that God-created part of human nature was to break out of our traditional theological notions of sex as simply a biological drive to perpetuate the species.

Those occasions when I actually invited a man to spend the night only confirmed what I had for so long suspected: We were not created to be alone. The sex act itself was, of course, a release. But to hold, caress, embrace another person through the night offered a glimpse of the wholeness in human life God intended.

The stumbling block came in the form of those dreaded "mornings after." What seemed like a wonderful idea in the haze of a smoke-filled club, especially after several rounds at the bar, dissipated dramatically when I would awaken next to someone with whom I had no emotional investment. The small talk over morning coffee, the awkward search for some common ground, and hastily scratched phone numbers before making a quick exit, all left me cold. Hollow. Some itch was not being scratched. Before too long I was back on the couch; this time with a therapist of my choosing.

I went, ostensibly, to work through family problems. Soon enough, though, it was to discuss sex. I remember my time with that therapist, not so much for what he did, but for what I said early on in our sessions.

"Oh no, I could never sleep with a woman," I said, responding to his question, "that would be *real* sex."

Thanks to my fundamentalist childhood, sex with a woman was sex. Sex with a man was, at best, fooling around. It was not real. Either society's categories or my religious training, or probably a little bit of both, had so formed me in my notions about relationships that I still did not believe that two men could be in love—romantic, passionate, committed love. So to have sex with a woman would imply something deeper, something more significant than just sex, something like love. To have sex with a man was simply being naughty. And being naughty meant feeling guilty. Even after years of hearing that Christianity is about grace and forgiveness, guilt was still its strong suit as far as I was concerned. It is perhaps one of the greatest tragedies of the institutionalized church that guilt is its primary by-product, sending countless unsuspecting converts to the therapist's couch. Which is why, I suspect, I became an Episcopalian.

I started attending an Episcopal church early on in my college days. A lot of the artsy crowd went there—students from the theater and art departments. I found then intriguing. They deviated just enough from the norm to be attractive. Besides which, I was sure some of them had to be gay. I remember wandering into that tiny Anglo-Catholic parish and feeling myself being drawn into a whole new spiritual world. People were kneeling, standing, bowing. Colors, sounds, and gestures filled the worship. From the very first sermon I heard in that place, the Bible suddenly became a source of life, that book that had terrorized me for so long. For whatever reasons, I immersed myself in that parish. What began as a fascination with candles and incense soon became a deep love for the sacramental approach to life. Hearing that the divine actually did penetrate the world around me liberated me from the over-intellectualizing of my past. Suddenly worship was not disembodied. What I had been discovering in my sexual awakening was being lived in a sacred space: Physical things mattered. I did not have to leave my body at the front door, nor all the desires and yearnings that make us human. God became flesh when I walked into that Episcopal church; after all the years of hearing it, I finally believed it, deeply. The rift between my body and that soul I had tried to lop off began to heal.

I started keeping a journal again.

Act III: God Calling

Oddly, looking back through my journals I cannot find any entry even resembling "I want to be a priest." And yet it seemed the most natural thing to do. My friends assumed so. The congregation where I attended church took it for granted. And the rector remarked, after telling him my plans, "I wondered when you would finally realize your calling."

Vocations are a tricky business. How does one sort out all the motivations? What words can one possibly use that are not cliché? How could I be gay and a priest? I was still not out to my congregation. I had not told my priest. I had only a small circle of friends who knew the real me.

Could I keep that circle of secrecy my whole life? How could I live a gay life and be a pastor? What sort of congregation would accept a man for their priest's "wife"?

Whatever the difficulties involved, I had to forge ahead. Perhaps, I thought, priesthood would fill whatever emptiness sex could not. Surrendering to God would make the church my family. Even if it meant celibacy, I would do it for the God who would not let me go. I would do it, ironically, for the God whom I had discovered loved all of me, sexual preferences included.

So I packed my bags, put sex on the shelf, and plunged into that never dull, zany world of seminary life. I promised myself never to speak of sexuality. The topic was irrelevant, as far as I was concerned. I would simply go to class, say my prayers, and leave amorous desires locked away.

Moving day. The dorm hall was littered with boxes and the debris of first-year seminarians adjusting to cubicles for living space. I had not been on campus more than an hour when I caught sight of Antony. More Italian than Ragu, he was, to my sex-starved eyes, a vision. He was unpacking a stereo that would fill more than a third of his small room. I practically fell against the door-post as I slammed on the brakes to take another look. After seeing his eyes, I knew I was in trouble.

God, the humorist, provided yet another distraction in David. As I was introducing myself to Antony, I heard a voice from across the hall, "My dear, how can you survive without your boas?" Thus began my seminary career.

My sexuality refused to be shelved. Within the first week Antony had invited me to his room for a bourbon, where, much to my delighted surprise, I spent the night. Little did either of us know that those cinder-block rooms might as well be radio transmitters. Antony's next-door neighbor could not have known better what was happening that night if he had been sitting in the same room. Fortunately, he was not inclined to broadcast the information to the general population, nor even to the Dean. Antony and I realized, however, that discretion is most certainly the better part of survival, if not valor, in a seminary community.

In the midst of a schedule packed with chapel services, classes, and studies, Antony and I managed to steal away for long walks, take drives into the country, or escape to a nearby faculty member's house for dinner—a place where gay students could feel at home. For me it was a taste of bliss; no more seedy bars or brushes with police. We would occasionally catch each other's eye in chapel, hold hands in the woods, and escape for a welcomed "real" meal in a city restaurant. The romantic in me was gorging himself.

We lurched through what was an increasingly stormy affair for about two months. We both began to realize that the fish-bowl life of a seminary makes such romantic liaisons impossible, or at the very least, stressful. We wondered who next would whisper behind our backs about how much time we were spending together. The anxiety of constantly looking over our shoulders when we went for walks soon took its toll.

Fortunately, there was David, the one who had not only forgotten his prized boa collection, but his brooch box as well, when he came to the seminary. As Antony and I drifted apart and finally broke it off, David was there to pick up the pieces, many of which had guilt written all over them. I could not seem to lose that fundamentalist baggage from my earlier years. It had not helped that my hometown rector had sent me a book that attempted to locate the origins of homosexuality in a distant father-son relationship. The book made some sense, and I began to wonder if maybe I had been journeying along a path of sin rather than liberation.

"Well, child, that was a popular idea about twenty years ago," David drawled with a leftover hint of Virginia gentleman when I described the book. "But if that's true, where's the origin for heterosexuality? A distant mother-son relationship?"

"I never thought of that."

"Obviously not. Let me tell ya' something. Everyone has to get through this stage. The guilt, the wondering, the regret. It takes some time, and a lot of prayer."

"Prayer?" Throughout our time in seminary together, I never ceased to be amazed by David's spirituality. He was definitely out, fun-loving, wild and crazy, and at the same time, a man of prayer and spiritual sensitivity, par excellence.

"Yeah, prayer," he went on. "For a long time I kept my sexuality out of view, back there in the shame-corner, you know? I loved men, but I was sure I was the only one. After a lot of time talking, and crying, with good friends and a university chaplain I finally realized I needed to go to confession."

"Confession? But I thought..."

"Let me finish, child, just hold on. I went to my priest and told him that I needed to confess my ungratefulness. Of course he didn't get my drift, so I told him again that I had not accepted my sexual orientation as a gift from God, and I needed to confess my ungratefulness."

I was amazed. Sitting there, listening to David talk about being gay as something to celebrate was like seeing a black and white movie colorized. It was a whole new world. Homosexuality was not something to be suffered through or merely tolerated, but embraced. Being gay was not a twist in creation, but a gift! Liberation: part two.

Summer came and it was time for Clinical Pastoral Education (CPE). It was a required program of chaplaincy internship, and I ended up in a New York City hospital where I hoped to work with AIDS patients. For so many of them, coming out was forced on them by the disease. As I shared in their stories, I was moved and exhausted by the abandonment, the isolation, and often, the incredible courage they represented.

The litany of pain that summer seemed endless. Michael was a success- ful Manhattan lawyer living in a posh Eastside apartment, gay, and deep in the closet...until that summer. When I first met Michael I assumed the terror that seemed to contort his pretty face was a response to his diagnosis. In fact he was about to confront his parents, who were on their way to the hospital. The prospect of informing his high-society family not only of his illness but his sexual orientation filled him with dread. And, I would discover, for good reason. They refused to see their son again until his funeral later that year.

Gary and Thomas (although I most certainly remember all the names from that summer, none of these are real) were a different story. They nearly basked in a remarkable pool of support from their families. I remember siblings, parents, and other friends visiting Thomas frequently in the Intensive Care Unit, and including Gary, his lover, in all the family decisions. The issue for Thomas was not so much a familial one, but anxiety over his work. He was a talented musician working for a Broadway show. I was simply incredulous to learn that the entertainment industry preferred denial to confronting the reality of so many gay men in the business. Thomas wondered how soon he would be replaced, even if he recovered from this particular hospitalization.

There was Jerry; well enough to be discharged but evicted from his apartment he had nowhere to go.

Gregory, as an IV drug-abuser and gay, had no family, and little help from the social services staff.

Leo could go home if only his lover had the time and the skill to see to his health care needs. He didn't, and eventually left Leo.

I was swimming, over my head, through a case-load of suffering. All at once I was confronting my own sexuality, the demons of fear and insecurity, and the whole question of my own mortality in the faces of my patients. And, not surprisingly, guilt paid yet another visit. How, I wondered, and ever more loudly as the summer wore on, could I be a pastor to these people who risk so much, and lose so much, while I stayed safely cloistered behind my closet door? How could I minister among the risk-takers without risking at least as much? If indeed a major theme of the Gospel is offering a voice to the voiceless, as I so firmly believe, then at the very least, I must let my own voice be heard or else face a ministry void of integrity.

To say that my three months of CPE was transformative is like saying the QE II is a rather large boat. I began by coming out to my colleagues in the CPE group. It seemed like a big step for me at that time even though our supervisor had already done as much at the beginning of the summer. But I realized it was not enough.

I had finished my first year in seminary a contented, albeit quiet, homosexual. I returned, after CPE, militant and angry. Pink triangle buttons were standard with every outfit. Gay liberation was the topic of term projects. Advocacy for PWAs appeared in my sermons. I attended the National March on Washington for Lesbian and Gay Rights, and made sure the seminary knew it. Feeling good about my own sexuality and standing up and speaking out for the silent minority not only brought a new freedom, but a deep sense of healing with my past. Perhaps pretentiously, but with every confidence, I felt I stood in line with all the great prophets of history.

With graduation approaching, the next step was clear. I had to tell my bishop. There was no turning back, and I could not bear the thought of living a double life once ordained. If the bishop could not accept it, he ought to at least hear it from me first.

After writing him a long letter, he asked to see me. All my old issues with those in positions of authority came screaming to life. This was my spiritual "Dad" I was dealing with. So what if I graduated with honors? Being gay might mean I still had not made the grade. I took some comfort from my past experiences with him, remembering him to be a pastoral and sensitive man. At least he would not, I believed, dismiss me out of hand. Admittedly, I was fairly confident our conversation would be positive, that he would be understanding. The uncertainty concerning my vocation was not nearly as terrifying as what "Dad" would now think of me as a person. I wanted to be loved and respected, not just tolerated.

I made the appointment. We sat comfortably in a couple of wing-backed chairs. My stomach was churning while we made the usual small-talk pleasantries until I finally said, "Bishop, I'm here simply to be honest with you about my sexuality. I don't want to do anything in this process that might even resemble deceit."

He paused long enough for me to hear my own heartbeat while he offered his well-worn inviting smile. He looked at me with a kind of penetrating gaze one expects of bishops. (They must learn that in bishops' school.) Gently and quietly he said, rather simply, "You mentioned a bit about your journey in your letter. Can you tell me some more?"

"Well," I started, finally exhaling a long-held breath, "it's not been easy, as you can imagine. I've known about being gay ever since I can remember. But until recently I've always felt I had to cover it up, keep it stuffed inside." My friend David's words from that night in seminary came to me. "But I have come to accept it. No, more than that, I have come to be grateful for it. Seeing my sexuality as one of God's many gifts has helped immensely."

"That's quite obvious from your honesty. I appreciate that a great deal. My experience with gay men in the past has been somewhat of a mixed bag." Well, I thought, here it comes, thanks but no thanks. "I have known too many gay men who have kept that part of themselves stuffed inside, like you said. What matters to me is whether or not someone is able to integrate their sexuality into the rest of their personality, be a whole person. That goes for both straight and gay. Treating our sexual selves as if they did not exist, or at best stashed away in some dark corner of our lives is never healthy. I have no problem with ordaining gay men as long as they are at least working toward that kind of wholeness."

Surprised, yet again, by grace. My sigh of relief must have been audible. That journey of wholeness was precisely the one I had been striving toward. Confident that the matter was now settled, I was wondering about the new wrinkle in the bishop's brow.

"You will, however, be going to a suburban parish," he noted rather somberly. "You need to be aware that your kind of honesty may not be as readily accepted there."

That puzzled me a bit. With the bishop's approval out of the way, what other possible hurdles were there? I would soon discover just how true, if understated, his comment had been, and how desperately naive I still was.

Epilogue: Risking a Human Face

From my theater friends I learned about the Muse, that faceless spirit which animates a play. They were intense about this spirit. Their constant struggle, both within and without the walls of the theater space, was to be real, without pretense, unabashedly human. They spent countless hours studying their characters, discerning their motivations, naming their feelings. As much as it lay in their power, they were to be that character; the lines of the play must have a human face. In that struggle, that quest for authenticity, the spirit they sought they named the Muse. Without that spirit, the drama could not begin. When the Muse is silent, the drama is only half human.

The human journey, the drama in which we all act, requires the Muse. When it is silent, we live our lives and speak our lines without a human face. For gay men and lesbians, the obvious first step is to let that Muse speak; to allow ourselves to hear deeply within us the voice that says, "You are different, but good nevertheless." For me it meant taking that lopped-off soul out of the locked drawer and owning it. It meant confessing to God my sin of calling bad what God had created good. To let the Muse speak is to allow grace, the Spirit of God, to flood into all the corners, seams, and crevices of human life. It means risking a human face.

The drama of my own life has been that never-ending search for authenticity. We do not come out just once. Each new job, every new social context demands a decision: Should I let the Muse speak? Coming out to my CPE group, for example, was relatively safe. Our supervisor had, after all, led the way, and I was confident I would receive the group's support. Other situations are not as easily sized up. How invested am I in receiving this particular group's acceptance? How will they react? How likely is it that word of my sexual orientation will spread beyond the confines of a particular group, and should that really matter? Will I lose friends? Make enemies? Lose employment?

It only takes one negative experience to convince someone that future decisions about coming out require, at the very least, caution. Following in my footsteps, one of my friends from college became an Episcopalian and joined my home parish. She and I had been close friends as students, so close in fact, that our friendship required periodic, rather intense reality checks. She saw us moving toward romance. I, obviously, did not. While the parish considered my application to be sponsored for holy orders, I felt the time had come to live in this friendship with more honesty. Not only to deepen our own relationship, but to begin my course toward ordination with greater integrity, I decided to come out to her, to risk a human face.

While she appeared to take the news better than I had imagined, she nevertheless felt compelled to inform my rector as well as several families in the parish of my "condition." Although the ensuing confrontation with the rector was not as disastrous as I feared, my relationships with a great many of those parishioners changed substantially. That change, while not directly oppressive or combative, was deeply painful. A large chunk of who I am as a human being, once revealed, threw me into a different light; a light that was strange, foreign, often unacceptable, and for some, repulsive. In that parish, risking a human face meant risking acceptability and belonging. When those are lost it becomes all too easy to slip behind the more comfortable masks and muffle the Muse.

So for me the drama has been inextricably bound up with God; with God and the Christ-drama. How can my story more fully reflect, and indeed incarnate, that story of God with a human face? Clergy especially seem subject to a kind of spiritualizing that wants to deny the human (read "unspiritual") condition. Wearing our colorful vestments on Sunday and locked behind austere collars during the week, presents a picture, an icon, of other-worldliness. We clergy are somehow different.

I remember an experience shortly after being ordained of wandering through the local grocery, cart filled with the usual potpourri of household litter. A parishioner walked by in the aisle, did a double-take when she saw my collar, and said, in a rather appalled tone of voice, "Why, Father, what-ever are you doing here?"

I looked around to make certain I was indeed in a supermarket, and then replied, "Well, I'm buying food."

"Oh, of course," she giggled, "I never thought of that."

I was tempted to add that the days of receiving manna from heaven (not to mention housekeepers in the rectory) are long since gone, but decided against it, smiled politely, and moved on to the personal hygiene section.

That simple incident provided my first taste of how deeply we Christians still insist on separating human from divine, spirit from matter, as if the Incarnation never took place. If the image of a priest buying groceries can evoke such incongruity, imagine how such people would react to learning that we even have sex drives. Even for our straight, married clergy with children I am sure there are those parishioners who would prefer to believe that those kids come from some magic baby-patch in the backyard rather than from anything as unsavory as sexual intercourse.

Maintaining that distance between human and divine is simply less messy, less complicated, less threatening. But if we clergy are to be separate and different at all, then at the very least we ought to be modeling what the Incarnation is all about: God with a human face. If we clergy can proclaim and live the story of a God whose dwelling is indeed with humankind—in, among, and through human beings and their relationships—then perhaps our congregations would not be so terrified of their own humanity. Perhaps then we clergy would not be raised above our churches like some giant, superhuman movie screen where our people project all their insecurities about being human. The union of human and divine in Jesus must speak to the deepest depths of our own humanity or it means nothing at all. But that requires risk, telling the story, unmuffling the Muse.

For everyone, gay or straight, this journey of liberating the Muse within each of us is at the heart of the Gospel. Theologically, it means healing that fundamental rift between "spirit" and "matter" which has, quite ironically, given the centrality of the Incarnation, plagued the Christian tradition for so long. The implications of such healing extend beyond merely feeling good about our sexuality. The Muse which has so long been kept silent not only can, but must speak to the larger community of faith.

Our experience as gay and lesbian Christians can offer the kind of wholeness in human community for which we all yearn. We have a story to tell, an emerging spirituality which must be heard if the unfolding pattern of the Christ-life is to blossom afresh within the church. I am not particularly proud of my past, one that is rather littered with promiscuous and indiscriminate sex. My hesitation to own that past does not, however, stem from my childhood belief that such acts will send me to hell. Rather, besides being imprudent in this era of AIDS, one-night stands provide little means in providing the kind of wholeness and intimacy in our relationships God intended.

Clearly, I would not side with the remains of our puritan heritage which asserts a distinctive distaste and judgment on any genital sexual activity outside of marriage. Likewise, I would not want to assign quick sex the status of some kind of definitive solution to the question of human intimacy. Somewhere between these two polar views there must be a middle ground; a place where we celebrate our sexuality in our quest for deeper communion, between ourselves and with God.

It is precisely stories like mine that, if shared within the community of faith, could open the horizons of human intimacy. At the very least, our gay and lesbian stories can return to the Christian tradition the important role our sexuality plays in living a whole, integrated, human life—our sexuality not being severed from our spiritual selves, but inextricably bound to it.

If nothing else, such an integration of our spiritual and sexual selves would remind us of the importance of human touch. How critical this is to the human journey is no more clearly articulated than by those suffering from AIDS, who are often deprived of nearly all human contact. I remember visiting a particular AIDS patient in New York. I was getting nowhere. He would not respond to any questions, and barely acknowledged my presence. I decided to leave, and as was my custom, I told him that I would be around if he wanted to see me, and I gently squeezed his shoulder. He quickly grabbed hold of my hand and began to cry; he wept like a baby. When he could finally speak, all he said was, "You are the first person to touch me in two weeks."

Contemporary society has so truncated the meaning of sexuality and constricted its appropriate expression that we have become firmly locked behind a door of individuality for which no key exists which our culture does not consider sinful or dirty. Indeed, society has forced those who have understood, or at least caught a glimpse of sex as something more than biological, into destructive relationships, sex-role game playing, and a promiscuity which is in actuality a search for intimacy.

We need look no further than the gay and lesbian community's response to the AIDS crisis to see modeled the kind of compassionate community of human beings—unafraid of "touching" the human condition—the church can and ought to be, but has so often failed to be. While in Washington for the National March for Lesbian and Gay Rights in 1987, I was profoundly moved to witness members of our community lift, carry, hold, comfort, and protect against the cold various persons with AIDS who wanted to attend the rally. Civic and grass-roots gay and lesbian organizations, much sooner than the church, led the way in offering a Christ-like, deeply human response to people living with AIDS. Somewhere, the church has lost its vision of St. Francis embracing the leper as an image that energizes and catapults us into the Gospel.

The gay and lesbian story, however, embraces more than sex. To unleash our Muse within the church can offer a perspective on scripture and church history which highlights the importance of relationship and intimacy. Traditional scriptural exegesis has so often emphasized sin, especially sexual sin, as the informing paradigm for interpreting the great stories of the Bible. Those stories have less to do with sexual sin (if at all) than with twisted human relationships based on dominance, power struggles, and inequality. The most obvious example (and the one most often used as a weapon against the gay community) is the Sodom and Gomorrah incident. The fact that our modern judicial system still employs the word "sodomy" for the crime of anal penetration betrays how far astray the church's interpretation of that story has gone. It ought to be clear that the story's crime is not homosexuality, but rape, an act of violence.

More subtle examples reveal the continuing threat which holds the whole tapestry of sacred history together. Cain murdering Abel early on in the book of Genesis, a story of jealousy and dominance, in effect, sets the tone for the whole of scripture. It is about relationships: Jacob stealing Esau's birthright; Moses engaged in a power struggle with Miriam and Aaron; the woman caught in adultery and brought to Jesus for stoning. These stories are about who has power, who is going to wield it, and who decides how that power is going to be used. They are about relationships, and the sin scripture wishes to condemn is the absence of mutuality and equality.

The feminist movement has rightly critiqued our society as one based on power struggles, what has been called patriarchal domination. This dynamic continues to shape our perceptions of what is "masculine" and what is "feminine" in such a way as to create a society in which rigorous logic, little or no emotion, assertiveness, competitiveness and direct forcefulness (all of which are assigned to men) are held up and lauded as the foundations of our culture.

This system of sex-role stereotyping not only oppresses women, gay men, and lesbians, but feeds the whole complex web of racial discrimination, inner-city poverty, even third world domination by first world corporations. Consider the many stories from the Gospel in which Jesus heals women, lepers, and "notorious sinners." The religious leaders of his day condemned Jesus for it and plotted to kill him. Who would take offense at healing unless those healed were not only the forgotten ones of a society, but the ones a society would *prefer* to forget? In a society which is based on separating and categorizing people based on who is "worthy" of social programs, or worse, who is expendable, gay men and lesbians must point to these biblical stories, own them as our own, and offer a new vision.

The gay and lesbian story can offer a vision of relationships, both personally and even internationally, which are not based on exploitation and rigid definitions of which party has power and control. The current call from conservatives for a return to "traditional family values" is really a call to maintain the kind of power balance implied by this system of patriarchal domination. Tax laws, insurance policies, even municipal ordinances all seek to retain the nuclear family as the basic unit of a capitalistic, and often oppressive, system. Gay men and lesbians must overcome these many judicial stumbling blocks and cultural customs just in order to love each other. And loving each other in the face of such oppression not only bonds our community more closely, but threatens a system which is not based on love, but power.

Certainly, distorted relationships exist among some gay men and lesbians. But there is a quality of relationship within the gay and lesbian community, by definition, that does not depend on the systems of patriarchal domination. As gay and lesbian Christians we can stand up in this society, and in our congregations, come out, and say, "I am not like that. My relationships are not based on such twisted perceptions of power. Let me show you another way to live and to love."

While some of my experiences of coming out have been negative, most have been highly positive, and in fact, avenues of healing. Being open about my sexuality in a clergy support group recently prompted one of the priests, straight and married, to be more open about his own insecurities with the masculine facade he feels our society, even the church, demands he present. His need for intimacy with other men has been in conflict with how our society believes men are "supposed" to act in relationship with one another. One of my best friends from college recently told me how much he appreciated having a gay friend. Simply by listening to my story he has been able to more fully own those qualities in himself which our society would label feminine: sensitivity, compassion, gentleness.

Offering to each other our vulnerability opens up new possibilities for human community. Gay men and lesbians, in coming out, can begin to dismantle the sex-role stereotyping and game-playing that keep so many of us enslaved to unhealthy, even inhuman, relationships. Sharing these stories, living them in community with one another, creates that nexus where we may encounter grace; and by that grace begin to live more fully as God intended.

As a priest and pastor I have found the truth of what I have written here all the more painful. While honesty may be the best policy, it also places a burden on others they may not be willing to bear. The gay and lesbian experience still threatens how our society has been conditioned to live and to love. My first few years as a parish priest have been in the midst of a suburban, upper-middle-class congregation. I have been pleasantly surprised by their willingness to look honestly at themselves. But I have also learned that when it comes to the bottom line they prefer masks. The whitewashed exteriors we paint for ourselves are less threatening, albeit less human, than the sepulchers we wish to hide.

Regrettably, I have taken several steps back toward that closet; I have muffled the once outspoken Muse. I find myself listening to jokes about gay men or lesbians without objecting, and even politely laughing at the punch line. Certain women of the parish have decided to ease my perceived loneliness by trying to set up dates for me with a cousin or daughter. Rather than offering the truth (i.e., inquiring about their nephews rather than their nieces), I simply make sure my calendar is booked. I think twice before speaking out on gay-related issues, and worry about sounding too strident in my advocacy for AIDS-related services and programs.

There has been no outright deception, but no complete truth, either, and for former "Mr. Militant" this has been nearly devastating to my sense of self. But further, by not sharing my story of a grace-filled journey toward acceptance and discovering God's love in coming out, I am depriving both them and me of opportunities for growth. Whether they are truly not yet ready to hear my story, or whether that is my own projection, I have yet to discern. While we have shared so much, this congregation and I, and have grown to care for and love each other a great deal, to keep from them such an important facet of my life is a constant source of pain and guilt. I am unwilling to risk a human face.

Thus I struggled long and hard with writing this piece. To risk a human face might also jeopardize the ministry to which I have been called. The irony remains, of course, that without the risk the ministry is only half-human. By writing this piece under my own name I would certainly be coming out, and in a way I had not done before. I would be coming out to them, yes, but unfairly, and without the respect they deserve of hearing it, human face to human face. Currently the choices the church offers gay men and lesbians do little to promote healthy, human community. Either we remain in the closet, afraid and lonely, perhaps clandestinely hitting the bars, while we watch our very souls dry up, or we live with integrity, out and in relationship, and watch as the vocations to which we believe we are called slip through our fingers, or at the very least, be severely limited.

The solution, not unlike during my college days, is to write this piece under a pseudonym. Like all the other names I have used in this piece, my name is not real. Like the "Diary of a Personal Problem," it feels too much like lopping off a chunk of that soul I have tried so desperately to heal, and not unlike betrayal; betrayal of all those who have gone before me and are currently risking their human face for the sake of the Gospel.

This solution then, as in college, is not acceptable. So the drama continues. Where next will I be able to let the Muse speak? How and when will risking a human face lead to a deeper understanding of the Gospel and not humiliation or the loss of employment? Is God perhaps asking me to risk that for the sake of the Gospel? The question has been with me from the beginning, and I suspect will be for years to come.

On retreat prior to my ordination, surrounded by the Gothic structures of a convent, I pondered these questions, and I let the Muse speak, briefly, on the pages of my journal:

Holy places: Time-worn spaces where the prayers of the earnest God-seekers and superstitious skeptics alike stain the walls like clouds of incense. Castle-like towers surround me in this place. The all too phallic-like steeples rise above this summer-baked ground as in a thirties movie.

Murder mysteries: Agatha Christie movie sets in which old mansions hidden by groves of gnarled trees conceal evil plots and the strange dynamics of people gathered to solve a mystery. The tumbled boulders that keep the lake at bay serve only to accent the plot; who next will be impaled on the whims and fancies of fickle human volition?

Holy places and murder mysteries. Are they so disparate? We are told to die to self, to let go, to surrender to that dark night of mystery and great cloud of unknowing we presume to call God.

Sex and priesthood. Are these so disparate? A "little death" orgasm is sometimes called. And we are told that ordination is a marriage, of sorts, a wedding of persons. And yet is it not closer to mortification in the eyes of some?

These walls, the stones and arches, the colored glass and worn paths, speak and recall the lives of holy men and women. Their blood flows through the aisles of this old chapel and my heart somehow yearns to hear them sigh or sing, groan or pray. But are their prayers the songs of the contented faithful, the ones who had encountered God and found rest? Or would I hear the wails of lament, the agonizing realization of lives spent and wasted, of loves lost, sacrificed to some twisted notion of a jealous God?

Holy murders and mystery places.

Does God really desire the death of what God created?

The answer must be no. God does not desire the death of any created thing, not even that Muse which is silent.

Jonathan Emerson is a pseudonym.

TIM MILLER

Jesus and the
Queer Performance Artist

*N*ineteen-ninety was a very strange year for me. I am a performance artist, a queer, and a member of the Parish Church St. Augustine by-the-Sea in Santa Monica, California. This year, I found myself in two very different and intense situations both pushing at each other in seeming contradiction.

I whirled around in the center of the nationwide media circus contro-versy surrounding the National Endowment for the Arts. Unanimously rec-ommended Theater Fellowships to Holy (ooops, that's HOLLY) Hughes, Karen Finley, John Fleck and myself were overturned by NEA Chairman John Frohnmayer because of the content of our work. You see, three of us were gay, Karen Finley was an angry feminist, and all of us explore sexual content and refer in very different ways to Christian imagery and archetypes as a way of exposing and healing the lies and hurt of our society. We all exist in a highly ethical and moral framework of compassion for suffering. We were being fashioned as sacrificial lambs to the great slathering mouth of the lunatic right wing of Jesse Helms and his ilk. Our work was shown on network TV, misrepresented in the major press, and lied about in Congress. It became clear we were being hung out to dry. This was in order to soothe the nutso religious right who need to see gay men, lesbians and feminists censored and vilified for speaking the truth about the pain and hurt in our land to Caesar and King George.

Cross fade to a few weeks earlier. I was part of the Mass at St. Augustine doing a performance art sermon with Priest Malcolm Boyd. This work, presented as the sermon for the 10:30 a.m. service on Passion Sunday, tried to interpret the intensity of Lent, Easter and the crucifixion in terms of social justice. Through humor, performance actions, and audience participation we asked the congregation to search their hearts in order to identify the ways we crucify one another through racism, homophobia, economic injustice, AIDS, and environmental disaster. Building toward a powerful chaotic moment, the performers in the congregation began springing to their feet in the pews, hurling and receiving insults and being both the crucified and crucifier. The craziness finished with a shout from a bullhorn recalling a peace mass Malcolm had celebrated in the Pentagon during the Vietnam war. The police-man who arrested Malcolm said, "You are disturbing the peace." I spoke over the cacophony, "This is my body, which is given for you. Do this for the remembrance of me." The sermon ended with Malcolm telling a story of an unexpected communion in a shack during the civil rights movement. I would break into the story with my genuine need to find the acts of love in this world. To find the gesture of redemption, whether that gesture is seen in an AIDS buddy or someone feeding the homeless. The point is that all of us put each other on crosses and are crucified. Malcolm and I asked the congrega-tion to make the crucifixion personal; to acknowledge the sacrifices, miracles, and evils all of us take part in. The performance art sermon was a charged event that moved and energized the audience who came that day to witness this happening and share in this fusion of liturgy and performance art.

Malcolm and I did disturb the peace that morning; but we also provided a journey for some folks through something strong. When the words "peace be with you" were spoken after the sermon, they carried a call and an urgency that was full of possibility.

I bring up these two events to pinpoint the strangeness of our time. The same year that I explore issues in my own faith as a Christian through a performance art sermon, I am also under assault from the Christian right for being a visible gay artist. This might be seen as an interesting model of reality for gay people who are culturally Christian and trying to create a new relationship to Jesus and this complicated religious tradition.

Okay. Honesty time. Enough with all the intellectual cum historical slash political hyphen contextual business. What is all this about? What do I actually feel about my Christian identity? I was raised with a lazy smattering of Sunday school, WASP spiritual cool, pro-forma golden rule, confirmation, and then out the door into my intellectual artist self. At the time, my strongest experience about the church I grew up in, the Whittier Hillcrest Congregational Church, was that on a youth group field trip to the beach I managed to make out with one of the other boys in a cave. It was a kind of epiphany, without a doubt.

It is so confusing...I feel that I was pushed away into exile from my Christian self. A whole part of my identity got left out in the rain. There I was devouring *Das Kapital*, Buddha's Four Noble Truths, teenage existentialism, and fellatio while ignoring Liberation Theology, the prayer of St. Francis, the love commandment, and the kiss of peace. Ooops. Why does this happen? It is certainly not uncommon. First, I was turned off by the blandness of organized suburban Christianity. Strike one. Then, I was driven away by the bloodstained history of inquisition, imagined heresy and conquest, those fucked-up oppressive parts of the tradition and the exclusionary signals that are sent to gay people by the bigoted religious right. Strike two. Finally, there seemed to be no way to incorporate my basically good feelings about Jesus into my post-adolescent intellectual/artistic/political hit parade. Strike three. You're out. Nothing personal, Jesus. I just can't stand the company you keep. It seemed to make more sense to chuck the whole thing. Get out of my face, Jesus.

A few tears (I mean years) later, the cultural crisis alarm bells start to go off. To go into hiding from my cultural and religious stuff is a tricky business for me. I clearly desired a spiritual underpinning to my life. This had led me to zazen meditation, Plato, and worship of Nature. Wanting the feeling of a higher power, I began also to search within my Christian self for the purpose of life and was moved by the message of compassion and social equality in the Gospel.

I have a desperate need to know who I am and to know where I come from. This means to snoop around the secrets in the attic and sift through your ancestors' faded papers that are stuck in a trunk somewhere in Kansas or Mesopotamia.

I am involved within a multi-cultural arts community where people from many different cultural backgrounds and experiences are creating art that helps articulate identity. This search often leads artists to their deep spiritual roots, whether an African-American exploring a connection to Yoruba spiritual practice or a Celt tapping in to earth-based practices of the tribes of the British isles. I need to understand why my heart and spirit are moved and illuminated by the need for renewal, the passion of sacrifice for social justice, the desire to find the way to love each other, the need to discover compassion as a building block for our culture. These are all spiritual needs that weren't really finding an answer in some of my art life and political activism.

In my work as a performance artist, themes that are clearly informed by a deep current of Christian identity keep coming up: crucifixion and rebirth, conflict and communion, epiphany and despair. The desire for moments of peace. Sorrow about the sadness in the world. A radical desire to ease suffering, my own and others'. For me, to finally comprehend these long hidden emotions led me to look into my heart and soul, as well as into my culture, to see precisely what was there.

Journal Entry 3/14/89

Things have gone completely crazy...everything in this art-life terrain feels up for grabs...I've never been more excited. I'm collaborating with Malcolm on what we are calling a performance art sermon. This has been a great experience. Dealing with my whole confused Christian thing. The weird text of performance artist and priest. Vocation. Shamanism. Lesson through parable. The sermon is going to deal with AIDS, the love command-ment, and social responsibility. St. A's is a great liberation theology type place. After the service last week Malcolm and I rehearsed on the altar. Making plans. Talking about the big stuff. What we want this experience to be for ourselves and for the parish. What is communion? The kiss of peace? It's making me deal with my long-suppressed Jesus stuff. Blood and body hey hey hey. Who is that guy up on the cross and what does he have to do with me?

* * *

I wanted to at least get on speaking terms with Jesus. This just seemed to make sense. But more important, it seemed to me that I needed to develop this relationship. The pressures of my world were pushing me into experi-ences of great spiritual challenge. The skinny guy up on the cross hits me stronger now after seeing so many emaciated friends wither away. I.N.R.I. over the cross has been replaced by A.I.D.S. over the hospital bed. The loss of so many friends and lovers to AIDS has pushed and aged me in ways I can't even begin to understand. The deaths of young men, whose bodies and spirits I had loved as much as my semi-retarded emotional abilities were able, has been an earthquake in the heart zone for me and my generation. Death scares me shitless. I have had to confront it at this early point in my life in a very powerful way. My friends and I have also had to create or rediscover rituals for burying our dead and marking their passing. This has thrown us back to our spiritual upbringing (if any) and meant a new call to re-create our relation to the universe and God/Goddess. For me, this also challenges me again and again with the question from my journal, "Who is that guy up on the cross and what does he have to do with me?"

Journal Entry 2/12/90

My first understanding of this Jesus guy is that he was a carpenter. This always made sense to me because I was always a carpenter, too. It just seemed reasonable to me that there was this dude long ago who made things, tables, chairs, useful things. When the church I went to as a kid was being built, I'd climb all over it with my friends. Looking for metal slugs. Saving them as treasure. Climbing up plaster stairs. Hiding in half-built steeples. It was like the holiness in the building was in the construction. The nuts and bolts of it. The nails and wood. I always felt good about the carpenter stuff since it was one of the few boy-type endeavors that I was real good at. That cutting, and smoothing, and building, was a good thing and probably a holy thing that rang true for me. And so it was good that Jesus was a carpenter and did those things too. I loved tacky biblical movies as a kid. There would always be those shots of chips of wood coming off the hand planer from a low angle as Ben Hur comes into sight on his way to the galley slave ships. Religious music, please, maestro. We would see Jesus only from behind, offering water to the sexy suffering Charlton Heston.

Later on...Jesus seemed to be much more something out of books. I was more comfortable with books because they were intellectual and appealed to my fat brain. Jesus hanging out with Alyosha Karamazov. Trying to understand his brother's parable about Christ coming back during the Spanish Inquisition and then having to be crucified again by the Grand Inquisitor. Jesus in the bathtub with J. D. Salinger as Franny and Zooey battle about trying to turn Jesus into St. Francis and then the final realization over the telephone that the fat lady with the big ankles is Jesus. All morality comes down to doing it for the fat lady...offering compassion and love. It was like these books, in my world that was built of such books, were the way to get at this thing...Alyosha and Zooey Glass became boyfriends, moved in together, and tried to make sense of the world.

Now...my hit on the Jesus thing...and the effort to try to get a sense of who he was...and what it means now. I get this mostly through Jesus as activist. The ways the mad dog message of love and social justice within the gospel Señor Jesus preached; resonates politically in Central America...or through Ghandi's Satyagraha...or Martin Luther King, Jr. and the civil rights movement. Jesus as a member of ACT UP. The crucifixion as the ultimate civil disobedience. This guy building chairs. Trying to create a reality where people actually might love one another. Getting ready to go on a game show, offering love to the fat lady in the front row. The Jesuit priests killed in San Salvador. They could have been me and my friends.

I have a need to short circuit my intellectualizing a little. I need to find the way to be with and comfort the dying, feel the pain in the world, confront my own fears and faults, listen to my heart and soul. All of us in some way are trying to live up to this big challenge to not treat each other like shit. This is a tall order. And, oh, the sorrow that I feel at the impossibility of the task.

* * *

So, this is where I am now. I have opened up a line of communication with Jesus and even found some part of me that is able to pray. I talk to him. Say hello. I have begun to heal a place inside me that was alienated and adrift from a deep sense of my family and where I come from, these strange northern European Anglo-Saxon tribes finding the way to bring their forest gods into the new religion from the desert. We mark the birth of the man who would sacrifice himself for others by bringing a cut tree into our living rooms at solstice time.

And, I am a carpenter. I have experienced feeling awe toward certain priests who have given their lives or labor for justice in El Salvador and other places and display a total commitment and faith and a willingness to work toward a world with a little less suffering and a little more compassion. This humbles my own well-meaning gestures. I approach Jesus as a friend and helper. He is someone I meet at an ACT UP action. He is there in the circle with us in my performance art workshop. He is part of the fellowship of my gay friends. I know his lips. He is around to help me find my way through the biggest challenges of understanding my own heart, the pain in my world, the Gospel as a social document, and the love commandment as an ultimate moral yardstick. We must love one another.

Meanwhile, I am still a performance artist. Still a sexualized gay man. Still a political activist working toward making this society start to work for the sick and poor, and open its arms to diversity. I have found a way to incorporate and include the part of myself that is Christian into my identity and creative work. I try not to close my heart to feelings of grace, forgiveness, fellowship. The times of the year have become more layered and powerful: the birth of the light at Christmas and the planting and resurrection of Easter. I am part of a community of artists, social workers, and political activists who are also Christian.

I felt that the two performance art sermons with Malcolm were the most controversial works I had done in terms of the community of artists and gay people. There was a strange sense of "Why is Tim doing this?" "This Jesus stuff makes me nervous!" "I just don't feel comfortable dealing with this Christian routine!" There was a feeling of simultaneous censorship: from the nutso right that I should keep my queer mouth shut, and from some people in the "secular" community of artists and intellectuals that I should soft-pedal the religion thing. Some people seemed to be saying, "It's bad enough if this is moving in your life, but can't you at least keep quiet about it, or at least have the decency to be a Tibetan Buddhist. Stick to Goddess worship, Buddy, or else!"

Whew! I know these are real questions. I know there are no easy answers. I am a gay man, yet I also am clearly connected to my self as a Christian. I love having sex; I am not monogamous. I believe in the healing power of sex and the role sex can play in creating communion in my body and spirit. It seems like Jesus and his friends were a passionate community of fellowship. Free from macho bullshit and focused on spirit energy. This is very familiar to the fellowships in my life. Jesus was ready to embarrass the idiots who wanted to stone the woman. This is a very important moment for me, the lesson where Jesus tells us to cut each other a little slack. This resonates for me as a gay man. It speaks to my heart as someone who has been vilified and attacked for being who I am. I love men. I love their bodies. I love their souls. I love their collection of characteristics, phobias, and geniuses, that makes them who they are. To be with a man physically is often to know him and value his personhood, and to create a communion and bond.

Journal Entry 10/18/89
Just in Minneapolis for an arts conference. Met a nice boy who was very cute from Philadelphia. He works at one of the artspaces there. He's also a performance artist, and he's doing a piece where he cuts down a big tree and then puts it in the gallery. He called it "the ultimate Duchampian ready-made." He was sweeter and dearer than this kind of art-school stunt would let on, though, and I felt a strong love for him and we were good to each other and had a sexy time. So strange, the last two men I've slept with (other than the boyfriend, of course): one cutting down a tree, the other, the refugee from Peru who works planting trees on Martin Luther King Boulevard. One a boy in a leather jacket smoking cigarettes, the other tye-dyed and recycling, and a faerie. I like them both. I love them both. A graceful and odd circle of styles and upper bodies...penises and souls...wardrobes and lifeforce. Between each other. Between them and me. I know my body and spirit better from my time with them. I feel closer to the world with them both in my heart.

＊ ＊ ＊

The first man I was ever in love with was Jesus. He was sweet. He was strong. He didn't play football or scream at me and he wore great clothes.

This feeling I had for him from a very early age is part of my love for other men. I imagine him as a generous and sensitive lover, ready to give and receive pleasure. I see him there for the other person. Rubbing tired muscles with all those sweet-smelling balms and ointments that they keep talking about in the New Testament. My relationship to Jesus is in a direct heartbeat to my gay identity. So for me there is not a contradiction. I feel firmly in line with the spiritual vocation gay men often feel that has been an enormous influence on the church and toward the shamanic impulse in other spirit journeys.

The man I have loved and lived with longest is not Jesus, but my boyfriend, Doug. Like Jesus, Doug is a Jew, a bit of a rabbi, and very much a troublemaker. We have shared the last cataclysmic eight years. His Jewish identity is very strongly defined both culturally and spiritually. Our connection is not challenged by the separation of our faiths. Neither of us excludes other metaphysical influences from our spirit lives, whether it be Jungian therapy or Sri Ramakrishna, Walt Whitman or Earth Worship. Our connection is not through what we don't share in specific cultural religious practice, but what we do share: the basic belief in a higher power and something outside ourselves that we can communicate with; that we find the way to honor the universe. It would be difficult for us if one of us had no kind of spiritual practice or foundation. That would be a conflict...a place with no dialogue. Our spirit journey is so intimate, so much a part of our relationship, that stereotyped ideas about a practicing Jew and Christian not getting along seem absurd. A moment where Doug and I recently waited to hear our HIV test results was an intense example of this. We were in about as existential a spot as I've been; Doug covered his head and prayed; I crossed myself and prayed. Our spirits were alive as these two queers called up Jesus/Goddess/Moses and anyone else who might help us at that moment, in that time of trial.

My identity as a spiritual person includes eucharist, zen meditation, sex between men, the Passover ritual, and planting my garden each year. The poetry and almost sexual intimacy of drinking the blood and eating the body of Christ connects me to the congregation, God, and the possibility for magic. The challenge of zazen, to just sit and breathe, tames my mind and craziness. The ritual meal of the Seder helps me understand my own liberation and flights from slavery. The miracle of planting seeds and harvest time tune me in to the cycles of life and death. My compost heap is another resurrection. All of these are part of savoring the body I am blessed with and the universe I am part of. All challenge me to nurture growing things (including my soul), and to work to care for our world and to ease the pain that exists.

Journal Entry 4/1/90

I have had a certain dream my whole life...or at least as long as I can remember. I am with a bunch of other people. We are connected by a kind of bond...a bond built on a work toward justice. I dunno...sometimes it's like a concentration camp thing...sometimes it's like that Andreyev novelette The Seven That Were Hanged, about friends who were rebelling against the czar and are taken out and hanged in the snow. Often, it's set in Burbank or somewhere like that. The shit has hit the fan...and people are being blown away.

We are there about to suffer and die...in this dream in all its forms...but there is a feeling of purpose and reason. If nothing else that we're trying to understand the world...why there is injustice and pain...finding a way to explain it...adjust...change...I dunno.

I think this has informed in the biggest fattest way my search through all my religious/spiritual/mega big-time understanding of the world. Whether it's the years doing and tuning into cool Buddha here in my Southern California polyglot spirit heritage, or more and more my vibes on Jesus...teaching...working...forgiving...dying...Why do we do what we do...how do we respond to the horrors of our time...the particulars...the Jesuit priests' brains smeared on the wall by fascists in El Salvador...Oh God.

I was climbing a mountain when I was about 17. I had hiked for about 200 miles with my brother through the Sierras. We had heard gunshots and screams the night before...It was probably just people fucking around, though we hadn't seen anybody for days. I got real scared...as scared as I had ever been in my life. I was sure I was going to die. I stayed awake all night in my sleeping bag, waiting for some crazed lunatic types to blow us away after mutilating us or something. Well anyway, it didn't happen and I finally greeted the day amazed that I was still alive.

My brother and I began to climb again before it was even light. Climbing...step by step in a very steep trail up a 2,000-foot rock face...I was feeling every molecule tingle and tune in to the miracle of being alive...reborn from my night of fear. I was ready for the big resurrection, the big satori, the goods were about to come my way! I was a great big satellite dish tuned in on God. Just send some my direction!

We got to the top of the pass. I expected some major chord epiphany, a brass band of the Virgin of Guadalupe...something...but there were just more mountains stretching as far as I could see, 12,000 foot tall mountains. I was pissed off. I threw off my pack and began to climb some more, up the sides of this path, throwing rocks down as I climbed almost straight up. My breath exploding, I climbed up another 500 feet. My brain pounding, almost bursting. Dizzy and angry and wanting, I got to the top and there was a big flat rock. I looked again and saw the mountains, and then *saw* the mountains, almost passing out. The big ecstasy, the big everything at once...lying on this flat rock at 13,000 feet with Jesus, and Buddha, and the old mountain gods of my tribes of the forests.

Whew it was all there...some kind of wordless thing...big voices...big feeling...and my heart getting as full as it's ever gotten...where my living and my dying were at the same time...my works and my death as one...the pain of Christ on the cross and a zillion acts of lovemaking through the ages as one...my life now and what is to come long after my body is feeding somebody's California poppies...and my breath quieted and I ate some peanuts and raisins, and then climbed back down ready to go back to the world.

* * *

It is not simple. The chasm that exists in my heart, in our society, and between one another, is full of pain. I have experienced this first-hand as I debate crazed neo-Nazis during this time of attention and controversy around my performance art works. There are many wounds that need to be healed. The battles around inclusive spiritual practice have pushed and challenged our society for two centuries over issues of slavery, the women's movement, civil rights, the war in Vietnam, and now lesbian and gay rights. The closer we can get to ourselves spiritually...and to find a generous place to include the diversity of our journeys, the sooner many of the hurts of our time may finally be healed.

For me, even as the hate-mongering of the religious right attacks me and my queerness, I still feel that I have my own relationship to God/Goddess and Nature. I will not let their hatred and racism and bigotry hijack Jesus to their polyester Bible Theme Park or make him a hostage in the Wedding at Cana water slide. Because I believe Jesus would be happier in bed with Zooey Glass and Alyosha Karamazov: planning to save the world, staying up late, talking philosophy. Making love.

Tim Miller is a performance artist, teacher and cultural organizer. His solo performance works have been presented all over North America and Europe. He is Artistic Director of Highways Performance Space in Santa Monica and is a member of ACT UP/LA (The AIDS Coalition to Unleash Power). His performance work Stretch Marks *has been published by the Drama Review/MIT Press.*

JUDY DAHL
Your People Shall Be My People

*T*he church was filled with little children. I was one of hundreds, filing into the pews of St. Thomas Church that schoolday afternoon. We were practicing for the upcoming Sunday morning when we would be receiving our First Holy Communion. The nuns had rehearsed this one part with us nearly six times, and my little seven-year-old attention span was by now out of bounds, as were those of many others. I knew—I could see it in their eyes—egging me on to begin the revolution.

Sister Mary Cyril caught my hand just as I reached to grab Patty's braid, eager to give it a mighty yank. Instead, Sister nearly yanked my arm out of its socket and whisked me violently out into the aisle of the church. She hushed the other children with an echoing slap along the inside of the nearest pew, which drew the attention of the others toward us. She pointed her habit-draped, angry arm up to the crucifix and staring into my now terrified, once revolutionary eyes, extolled, "*You* did that to him!"

I remember the long remorseful journey back to my place in the pew and the numerous additional times we rehearsed our potential journey to the communion railing. By now I was certain I did not deserve to receive the little gift Father would give me in just three days. Patty was happy. I stole a look at Sister Mary Cyril and saw her gloating over the stalemate of my revolution.

In that moment, I received the gift of my Catholic heritage which would follow me into the deep ravines of a spiritual quest: GUILT, the gift that keeps on giving. It had given me so much already. My mother was not a Catholic.

She was only an extremely devout Methodist. I was told she couldn't go to heaven with me. I had better pray harder for her. They say you can pray a person like this into heaven if only you could be good enough. That in and of itself was a weighty task, as I was also told I had been born with this indelible mark on my soul because Eve gave Adam an apple and he ate it. These people were my first parents and they blew it, and now my mom turns up Methodist, and the priest can't give her communion at a table set only for Catholics, the only potential citizens of heaven. Lucky for me she wasn't Jewish because they told me those people killed Jesus. Sister Mary Cyril hadn't heard that, apparently, because she seemed certain I had done that when I went to yank on Patty's braid. Confusion and guilt were growing in my school setting and it seemed to be spilling over into my home life.

My twin sister was born with a problem heart, and I no doubt had something to do with that. My grandmother told me it was all my fault when we went the state fair that Sunday. I had picked up a pretty pink balloon for my sister, who was at the doctor's with my parents, and was taking it home to her because she was unable to get one for herself. In the back seat, coming home from the fair, I was talking to my pink balloon friend when all of a sudden, in a burst of childlike play, I bounced and the balloon popped on the ceiling of the car. Grandma turned toward me and told me that I had broken the balloon and that would break my sister's heart. Ill-equipped to understand this, I revisited the crucifix again in my mind. It must be true—seems I can't move a step from Calvary.

Again and again the theme of guilt seeped into my childhood, leaving me lost in a sea of impossible feelings. Fortunately, there were many kind nuns in my early years. One told me about Saint Jude, the saint of lost causes. Little did either of us know she had given me a kernel of salvation. I began a vigilant commemoration to Saint Jude in an attempt to eradicate my impossible feelings. From this perspective, that gift may have been a great one, for it has led me to embrace women in a number of ways.

Days, even weeks, went by and in a visit to another parish, there was a statue of Saint Jude. I remember the first time I knelt before the statue, and the kind of longing I had to see a saint with pretty dresses and a smooth face. I remember looking at Saint Jude, wishing he could look more like Sister Terese. I have no idea where these thoughts came from, if not from within my very spirit. If I was going to deal with impossible issues for me, I needed a woman to rely on. I wanted softness and beauty. Early on in my vigil to Saint Jude, there was something in my very nature which called me from this male focus in my prayer life to a figure with which I could more closely identify.

In the second grade, my grandma died and my sister and I had to go to school anyway and "be brave because grandma was with God in heaven."

One very kind sister hugged me when I answered her question, "What's wrong, Judy, you are so quiet this morning." I couldn't help it; as hard as I tried, I began to cry as I told her, sobbing, "My grandma died this morning." What I didn't tell her, what I had no words for at the time, was how much I had hoped that my prayers to Saint Jude would have worked for me before she died. I so wanted my grandma to know that I was a good little girl, and I didn't mean to break my sister's heart.

After the funeral and the hush around grandma's name, I went to church and saw the statue of Mary with different eyes. My grandma's name was Mary, and I decided to pray to her to heal my young revolutionary spirit.

Of course I felt a heaped-up kind of guilt the first time I knelt to pray before the statue of the Blessed Virgin Mary. Would Saint Jude be angry with me? Would this break his heart? But there was a softness in all the stories and the music I heard about Mary. She would talk to Saint Jude and make everything right with him. There was definitely something different about praying to Mary. She had such a kind smile on her face. She seemed to be looking right at me. Sometimes I would have to put my eyes down. She seemed to know something about me that was good, maybe even salvageable. I liked praying to her. It made me feel good.

Once I had an ally against guilt, I felt more freedom to move around in the world. I became close friends with one of the sisters and began to feel more like heaven was attainable. Sister Marie became my closest friend and confidant. Our friendship was a pivotal connection for my spiritual and social development. She was the most certain reason I would later choose to enter the Benedictine Order.

It is customary for nuns to be transferred on a regular basis, and so it was inevitable Sister Marie would be transferred. After five years of one of the most influential relationships of my life, her leave-taking was extremely difficult for me. Her absence created an enormous void in my life. It felt crucial for me to fill that emptiness.

After Sister Marie moved away, Sister Terese and I began to spend a great deal of time together. I had known Sister Terese for many years, but my first allegiance was always to Sister Marie. Once Sister Marie was gone, I began to spread some other wings of my personality. Now that I was in high school and in a different school, it was easier and more acceptable to be close to the sisters from my grammar school. I had feelings well up inside me for Sister Terese which were unlike any I had experienced. We became close friends, and then our friendship began to take a shape which would change me forever.

Sister Terese told me she was leaving the Order. It was just about the time I was considering a religious life for myself and it came as quite a shock. I spent countless hours with Sister Terese as she prepared to leave the convent. My intentions were pure but my feelings were all over the place. I was only partly in touch with who this woman was in my world. I remember how I could sail in my mind for days with the memory of her smile. The truth is, I was falling in love with her, unlike how I had fallen in love with Sister Marie, that innocent, genuinely compelling bond of friendship which took me closer to my own heart. Nor was it like falling in love with Mike Randall, the little boy down the street who took me to the eighth grade dance. I stepped on his feet all night long. This was different. I was scared and exhausted from these new feelings.

Many times I waited quietly in the back of Sister Terese's room until all the kids had retreated from her eighth grade class. I would drive from my high school to spend those after-school hours with her and steal precious, hidden moments together. We would move in and out of being close in ways neither of us had been before. It felt so good to hold her in my arms. I would stroke the coif fitting snugly around those curls she was now letting grow beneath her habit. Daily, the gestures of affection gave way from guilt and moved into territory previously undiscovered by either of us. One Saturday, as she cleaned the last drawer of her classroom, marking the final chapter of her decade-and-a-half of celibacy and secrecy, our lips found each other in a frighteningly warm, forbidden moment. In the moments that followed, we worked hard to find comfort, absolving each other in awkward gestures, convincing each other in silence that our lips and eyes had met in a benign passion, a friendship with depth. We filled the remainder of our time together that day in silence.

I suppose we tried to believe the break in time until we would see each other again would hush the memory. We kept our activities pure for the next several days. We shopped for her new clothes. I took her to the beauty parlor and stood with her beside the mirror as she brushed her cheeks with the first hint of color they had known for nearly fifteen years.

We had spanned four days since that moment of intimacy. I had wrestled with guilt in ways not known to me before. I had rationalized, agonized, and waited with enormous amounts of guilt for the moment we would be alone together. Finally the day came around for me to pick her up at the side door of the convent. I was just six months from going into the very Order she was leaving, and my heart was filled with confusion. I seemed to be going in two different directions: the way of the spirit and the way of the flesh. While my body trembled, I was glad for the time I could absolve the guilt I felt for what I wanted with a life of prayer. When I touched on my truest feelings I found this reservoir of passion for Sister...oops, Sandra Lane. I was mostly overwhelmed by how beautiful she looked as she made her way to the car. Looking back, I couldn't keep my emotions in their place. I felt beyond myself an ever enlarging, drumming whirlwind of passion.

Her flight would not leave until the following morning. I had made reservations for her to stay at a motel near the airport. On the way, we stopped to see my mother, who gushed at her beauty and sent me on with her, assured that her daughter was a good Samaritan. I think she was glad for Sandra in my life, possibly hoping with some last hope that perhaps her leaving the convent would steer me away from the cloister doors.

Sandra and I made it through lunch, talking little of her past. She was thrilled as she stood staring at an open book beyond the cloister. Her love of me as her helper and friend flowed freely. We had avoided any proximity during the days before, thinking we must, unsure of what would follow. Yet, as we pulled up to the motel, there was a drive, a powerful, organic, dynamic lunge from within us both which pushed aside any guilt—even the fear of hell—as we reached unabashed for each other on the other side of that motel room door, there we found a quick necessary path into each other's arms. That night in bed, we began our closure of what we had begun days ago. We spoke of friendship and the rightness of our compassion; and a deserved and well-understood, lingering goodbye. Wouldn't God want us as friends to be close in the moment of transition? Wouldn't it be received as an offering of love? We both knew, without sharing these thoughts, that our lusting bodies, moving over and beside each other were the only answer we could cherish in this sacred time of common-union. We had a precise code of morality, careful not to touch where the moistness of our bodies flowed. But we were freer now with our kisses. Hungrily, a woman from the reign of celibacy and a young virgin moved toward the future. Our joint escape into sexuality absolved by genuine love and human need, left us separated at the airport, my not knowing where this would take us, so great was the guilt which banished us from each other. "Entreat me now to leave you or to go from following you...."

Leaving the airport that morning, my mind took me back over the past several days. I cried deep billowing sobs for what Sandra and I had experienced and for what was left unfinished. We had come so close to something strange and unknown and still inexperienced in my young life. She had been a partner toward intimacy. My teacher, my friend, my spiritual guide, had led me to the door of the flesh and abandoned me to deal with a battered spirit overwrought with guilt. Could it be that this insatiable gift would follow me into every bed, every dream, throughout eternity? My mind wandered in and out of the quiet places I had known in the past few days of passion. I recognized it as a place in me that could never be understood, too forbidden to confess, too grand to grieve, too huge for the young semi-virgin I now knew myself to be. I took these feelings into myself and held them close. They felt strangely like the deep reverence I knew in my prayer life. Holding Sandra now in a fresh memory just hours from the womb of our secret love, the holiness I had known in prayer, the quiet, deep connection I felt with the divine took on new and heightened meaning as this experience of love and passion washed over me with the same kind of warmth and hope for a God, a life, a love, a meaning greater than what I had known.

The first time I felt this was shortly after the interruption of my revolution during our practice for Holy Communion. I left that day convinced of the great need in my life to wash away my sins by becoming a holy child. I heard holiness was a key to the door of heaven. The saints were holy. I began then to seek holiness.

My sister and I both received little books for our First Holy Communion. Our grandma gave us each a rosary. We spent the Saturday before our First Holy Communion wearing a path in the carpet from our bedroom to the living room as we diligently prayed the rosary and read aloud the prayers printed in our little missals. Mother looked miffed at this instant changeover. Just days before, we had been two very normal, clamoring, inquisitive seven-year-olds. Since mother had not heard the "braid story," she could only surmise that this was kind of phase, something which would go by the wayside with time. The intensity of that day did diminish the great need for moving off Calvary, but the bud of holiness had been planted and followed me for years as a search for peace and quiet.

Almost simultaneously, leaving the saint of lost causes and finding the Blessed Virgin in her soft, smooth, accepting manner, came a rush of other woman saints. There was Saint Theresa of the Little Flower, whose life story taught me to keep Jesus first and all else would come as I needed it. I spent hours lighting candles before her statue and worked diligently to please her and to emulate her. As my confirmation day came around, it was her name which I added to my own as I chose my confirmation name. She touched a deep void in my spirit. She took me to heaven in my prayer life. I could pray for hours beside her and believe with every fiber of my being that she heard me. I began a novena to Our Lady of Perpetual Help to continue to root out of me that self-willed, independent revolutionary I continued to feel surge inside.

Every Tuesday night for seven-and-a-half years, I went to do a novena. I never missed! There was this depth of holy oneness I recognized in my prayer with these heavenly women. I spent hours and hours of my life gazing into the porcelain eyes of women whom I longed to emulate. I read their stories, prayed to them and for other people with them. I talked to my girlfriends about them.

I went to an all-girls' Catholic preparatory school and we spent days and weeks preparing for the crowning of the Blessed Virgin on May Day. One striking blow for me was the fact that I had not yet attained the kind of holiness necessary to crown the Virgin. I was only the vice-prefect of the sodality at my high school, and I looked on with glistening eyes as another girl was crowned the Virgin during my senior year in high school. I continued to go to Mass daily. Some days I went twice, some Sundays three times. There was something undeniable about the good feelings I had spending time with the nuns and the other girls in the school and the woman saints and Mary. I felt one with them as we all paid homage to this ancient rabbi who was the beginning and the end of this prayer and holiness. Christ was a word in our prayer, the center of each ceremony, reminding us of our ultimate purpose as he gazed from the cross. Yet our community of women and saints and his mother had become a threshold of holiness for me which meant real life, beyond and before the cross. I was coming to understand that I could only know life more fully if I too entered the cloister and moved behind the walls of the Holy House.

All the "ejaculations," which were short quippy little one-liners which we spoke in church and to ourselves as good Catholic children; all the many "pagan babies" we had purchased with our prayers, oddly and wrongly purchased as the imperialistic answer to some Roman bishop who thought children from other parts of the world could have no other access to heaven; the many genuflections and rosaries and novenas had brought me to a place of holiness, a place of piety, where at seventeen I understood to be a path to religious life.

All holiness aside for those last few hours before the entrance I would make into the Benedictine Order of Nuns, I smoked my last pack of cigarettes and wore crazy clothes and had a generally rowdy good time. By today's standards, I was a wallflower, already a nun in every sense but one: I had slept with a woman, I had held her and she me, and I walked those memories into the convent with me that day.

I knew even before entering that one of the first lessons I would hear was the admonition to stay away from "particular friendships." As my particular friend of many years, a woman who had mothered me during the rebellious teen years when I would not allow my own mother closeness, drove me to the priory, I recaptured in an instant the years before in which guilt and holiness had played such equally vital roles in my life. I gazed out the window, eager for the newness ahead and grateful for the formative years I had, for all the holy women I had known (both the heavenly and earth creatures who had given so much in their memories and their lives to my roots), and my destiny. In some very certain though hidden ways, even then, the male creatures in my life—yes, even Jesus and God the Father—could never go with me into the next phase of my life. It was of its own definition in the very institution which established it, a place for women to be apart from the world.

As Sister Marie drove me to the Motherhouse that day, the spires of the convent chapel came up on the horizon and my attention was drawn to my lifetime friend now driving me to the priory. I remembered her from the morning of my First Holy Communion, where it seems now, so much of this began for me. She was there then, though younger, my particular friend, in the very truest sense of the word. She was a sister in this Order, yet I would be asked to leave her behind as I entered the convent. So well prepared had I been for this moment, with guilt and holiness my partners, I faced Sister Marie and we left with the friendship of so many in the quiet, echoing halls of my new home.

"...for where you go I will go and where you lodge I shall lodge;..."

Just moments separated me from the rest of my life. Now, sitting in a room with virtual black and white strangers, I found myself still lingering on the morning of my First Communion. What had that been after all if it was not the blending of two spirits in a spiritual relationship? Wasn't that a taking in of the Christ, the Other, the greater, my victory over guilt, my link to holiness? Had that not, in fact, been the first moment of spiritual relating in an intimate form?

Looking down at the folded, slightly trembling hands of a young seventeen-year-old woman, I realized I had left behind every hint of understanding I had to this point in my life. I knew in a moment of sheer panic that what I had based my entire spiritual life upon had been in the relationships I had formed with others. With my sisters and my mother and the sisters and Mary the Mother of Jesus, and Jesus to a lesser degree, and my women friends the saints, and now, as I turned back in the direction of the mistress of postulants, I was hearing what I knew would shatter my formation, "Stay away from particular friendships."

I had more ways than even I could have imagined to weasel my way out of the interpretation of what constituted a "particular friend." There was no question in my mind but that Sandra had been a "particular friend." I managed to set that experience aside and deal with it as a passing fancy, a phase.

There were only a few days a month we could receive mail. All of our letters were censored. Most of my girlfriends from school were also in the convents. We were spread out over the country in five or six different settings, depending on the Orders we entered. One of my closest and dearest friends had entered the same Order as I just the year before so we would catch a glance of each other occasionally.

I couldn't help but remember our popular escapade when she was a senior and I was a junior and we climbed into the window of the convent near our high school, took the habit of our school principal to the cleaners and had it box pleated! We were so proud of ourselves, until Monday morning when Sister Francis called the two of us into her office for discipline.

How could she have known it was us? She said she would never have thought of anyone else! The guilt—seems I kept a hearty supply available in my memory.

My memory often took me to the relationships I had formed throughout my high school years and my friends who had each been particular in their own way.

One winter night, after a cold, blustery walk across the grounds of the priory from the refectory to the dorm, I wrapped myself in my warmest bed clothes. Soon after getting under the covers, I felt a warm body crawl into my bed with me. I had earlier been giggling, quite inappropriately, with one of the other postulants and I thought she was going to continue the invasion of the "grand silence" by getting into bed with me to get me to giggle. Yet, as I turned to face my intruder, I found Sister Benjamin, a novice, who had crept up from the novitiate on the floor below to see me. She told me she was cold! I was truly stunned and asked her with a quiet kick to get out of my bed. I lay there all night long, unable to think of anything else. I seemed to be heading down some God-forsaken path with only the memory of Sandra as a pitiful guide out of nowhere.

And it got worse, or better, depending on what side of my life we are looking at.

One evening, I went to my priedieu and found a holy card from Sister Michael. It was a fairly benign spiritual card with a message of love in Christ written in her swirling cursive. The following night there was another, yet this time an almost cryptic message lured me into days of wondering. The holy card was a message from Dag Hammarskjöld, which said, "Life only demands of you the strength you possess. Only one feat is possible—not to have run away." I've kept that card all these years.

The following visitors' day, because I was so far from home, I was allowed to spend an hour with one of the professed sisters. Sister Michael requested that visit with me. Just the thought brought back some memories of a night not too far in the distance with a woman named Sandra. I felt like a schoolgirl meeting with my new suitor. I only half expected that my convictions about her were true as she was so holy, so blessed, so beautiful.

She met me at the side door (there is something about side doors to convents, I know!). We walked close, hardly knowing each other except through glances, during prayer, while walking back from communion, a few shared meals in which we had been able to sit beside each other and gather small vestiges of each other's lives. She was handsome, tall, bright.

My heart raced unruly and beyond me as our hands would brush during our walk up to the hillside. There, a beautiful bluff overlooked a still, empowering ravine near the Motherhouse. She took me to her favorite spot, just beyond the garden to Mary. We laughed as we shared favorite stories.

She looked longer and deeper into my eyes than I knew how to ignore. I cherished the brief moments during which I could capture the profile she offered the world. Her face seemed chiseled from clouds, with softness that reached deep inside her soul...and mine. When she would turn her head again to me, I couldn't help but see those porcelain eyes I had stared into for so many years in my home church, begging the Virgin to rouse me from my guilt. That day I did not have the courage to beg. I was wanting to stay holy, wanting so desperately to obey the rules of Saint Benedict. But she offered me a smile, and then her hand, and I found my head in her lap as she gently stroked my hair and sang a song to me. I lay there only briefly without guilt. And then, like a flood of disproportionate strength, I knew that I, that we, had crossed over to the other side of friendship. She never touched my warm thighs or felt my racing heart in an embrace, but we knew in the meeting of our eyes as the visitation bell rang, that we had a profoundly spiritual and yes, sexual (God forgive us) connection.

Days passed between us with agonizing slowness. It would be weeks before we could come together in our quiet closeness. I could only think of her. That, of course, was why we were not to form these insidious particular friendships. Instead of my mind being centered on Christ, I found Sister Michael in every prayer, in all my classes, firmly carving a sinful hole in my heart.

The guilt from my past Catholic upbringing had been well served. As the weeks went on, I felt tortured by her until I made my way, shortly before my primary vows, to my new novice mistress to confess this sin of my particular friendship. I spent weeks in penance. My lusting flesh had served as an impediment to my vocation.

Sister Michael was present for my reception into the Order. She stood behind others who greeted me warmly and welcomed me. She kept her head to the floor, for she knew I was making way only for holiness as I entered this new way as a cloistered novice. That night during compline, the final portion of the divine office (which we recited daily), I found another holy card from Sister Michael. She was fond of e.e. cummings and chose a poignant message from him for me: "no time ago, or else a life, walking in the dark, i met Christ Jesus. My heart flopped over and lay still as he passed, as close as i am to you, yes closer, made of nothing except loneliness." I still cherish these cards as holy, wholly, creating and re-creating images of the power of love.

In the year of my novitiate, there were others who left holy cards, some of them with other intentions or friendships deeply camouflaged. I began to see in myself, a distant theme, a longing, aching, screaming woman, eager to move beyond the rules of the church.

Time and again I prayed for courage to pass over this confusion, this dissonant cymbal in me. I prayed for a release of the feelings I had to form particular friendships, but it would come back to haunt me. After all, it was here in the intimate moments I had with my woman friends that I felt most holy, most connected, most divine, and guilty on all counts.

I left the convent in a familiar whirl of confusion, unable to keep myself from a desperate wish to have just one more visit with Sister Michael. I had no idea how I could change our time together, but I knew I wanted more. My only salvation from myself, it seemed, was to move back into the normal mode of human living, away from this temptation. If I left the convent now, surely the church would be there to support me as I journeyed on. "Your people shall be my people and your God my God...."

Leaving was harder than entering had been. There was something about a community of women which had lured me to the highest goals I have known: a life of prayer, serving God and others. I had no idea where to go from there.

My first months home were spent getting used to the noise. I had no idea the world was so filled with noise. I stayed home with my parents for several months, then took off for a new life with a great job as a flight attendant. All the jokes about the "flying nun" ran rampant for many years. What I managed to keep secret for several years was the hidden life I lived.

I remember my first day in training, looking up at the instructor, and how her eyes caught mine. Were those porcelain eyes? I studied very hard during training. I went to Mass nearly every day and sometimes twice on Sundays if I wasn't on a flight. Toward the end of training, it was time to find a roommate and a place to live. I was invited to live with my instructor.

Shortly after my last check flight, Jill, my instructor and now soon-to-be-roommate, asked me if I wanted to go out for an evening. We did. We spent most of the evening sitting in her car at the end of the runway watching the flights come in, sharing stories from our earlier lives. She was intrigued by my convent years as she also had a Catholic upbringing. During this first night out together, she called me sweet names and allowed her hand to rest on my knee or my thigh from time to time. She spoke freely about the vice president of the airlines, whom she was dating. There was that familiar confusion in the air again but we were certain of ourselves. We didn't cross the line, not until she turned on the key to the engine and whispered so softly under the roar of the landing plane, "I think I'm falling in love."

I ignored the remark, while thanking God for all the noise in the world. I didn't sleep that night and graduation came too soon to find another roommate. She sensed my confusion and invited me to attend Mass with her the following Sunday. I went. It did my heart so much good to kneel after communion and touch base with the holy, stable spot in my life. But the relationship between us had a great deal of room now in which to grow and be nurtured. We lived together!

There was a growing physical sense in me which desperately wanted to have all of this come together and make sense. Yet there continued to be the voice of antiquity leading me from such a "vile" relationship and an experience of my convent years which served to underscore my need not to let Jill take Sandra all the way. But being human finally found its way with me. I was soon to know unequivocally, as would my mother and all others, that this was not just a phase.

Jill drove me to my hometown to pick up my car. It was a couple days' drive, and my hands and thighs grew moist with a growing sense of longing for Jill. I was beyond caring about what it would mean later on. I was terrified but eager, confused but desperately desirous. During one particular stretch on the road I put my head on her lap and closed my eyes. Not long afterward she gently laid her arm across my side and then, so as not to wake me if I slept, or frighten me if she had mis-read my hungry signals, she began to caress my breasts, first one and then the other, so gently and softly I could only muffle my deep breathing for a few moments. We pulled over to the side of the road and our lips strangely yet anxiously met in a lingering, heart-pounding kiss, and then we quieted so as not to steal the moment in a rush.

That night we roamed each other's bodies with our eyes. We could not speak. We each took our own silent corners and trusted the other with just so much of each other. We slept before we met each other in ways which were still uncertain.

The trip continued, filled with passionate kissing and guarded touching. We still had not sinned. We had maintained that deeply ingrained cavern between the flesh and the spirit until the following night.

She had a fire going and wine beside the bedstand. We both knew that we would never leave this evening the same. We would be changed, we would have experienced the forbidden. She slowly undressed me, never dropping her gaze, and then it was my turn and all those years before me faded into the eyes of my beloved. I gathered her in my arms. The angels and the women who had loved me as far as we could go had taught me how to physically love a woman. All the years of connecting spiritually and with untangled passion had been a training ground. Now tangible, physical gestures of loving played lazy teasing games in moist wet areas which had been untouched in me and touched only by a man with Jill. We loved through the night and into the morning. And then we loved through another day.

When it was Sunday, we went to communion. I had a brand new understanding of a sacrament—and forbidden fruit—and w-holiness. I knew now the meaning of God's love in real and previously inexplicable ways. My body and my spirit would blend in those first moments of lovemaking and restore my soul.

It wasn't until Jill left me that I was seared with a raking guilt. Nearly a year down the road, the impassable road for someone like me, it had become painfully clear to me that there would be no support for me from the church or from my work or from my world.

We had never admitted to being lesbian, because we weren't. Lesbians were perverted in their love and queer in the world. We were not, we simply, deeply loved each other. We knew to hide our secret, but we refused to name it or choose it. It wasn't until several years down this road that we, on separate roads with different lovers, began to embrace the reality of our love and life together.

That was twenty-two years ago. Since that time, I have come to know and accept myself as a lesbian. I now understand my confusion to be an indictment of the church, a church which has misunderstood the meaning of Christ in the world today. For in our human, sexual, sensual selves, lives the breath of a spirit which connects us and leads us to love, to our divine selves. My life had been an endless contradiction of faith until I affirmed the rightness of myself as a lesbian. I was forced from Christ, from the church, from my human community by guilt, and I found myself in the arms of women who would lead me back to myself.

Again and again my journey takes me back to the day of my First Holy Communion where in bold human, physical ways, God seeks to blend the human and divine in a dance of intimacy and common-union. In the Catholic Church it is seen as a sacrament, a ritual set apart from worldly offerings to create in us clean and worthy spirits. A sacrament where love moves beyond human understanding and touches the deepest recess of our lives.

As a lesbian, this communion, this blending, also unfolds again and again as one woman spirit meets another in the breath of lovers. I now understand this to be the unique, sweet "indelible mark" on my soul. For this I am ever grateful to my God, and my sisters.

> *"...where you die I shall die, and there will I be buried."*
> Ruth 2:16ff

Judy Dahl was born in Phoenix. She is an identical twin. She was raised a Roman Catholic and had 12 years of parochial education. She entered a Benedictine convent after high school. When she left the Order, she flew for a major airline for 12 years. She came out as a lesbian and struggled for years with her sexual and spiritual self. In 1976 she became a minister and graduated from the Iliff School of Theology with her Master of Divinity. She has served MCC in many capacities and is currently an HIV counselor. She is the author of River of Promise, *which chronicles her life with her partner of ten years and adopting their 2 children, who are now 2 and 3 years old.*

JAMES LANCASTER
Tales From Myself

*T*his is a secret. Most of this I have never before told anyone. I will deny every word. Eat this book when you have read it.

I was raised in Southern Baptist Sunday Schools in Southern California. There I was taught stories even a child could not believe. It wasn't just that the Bible stories themselves were preposterous, the teacher's interpretations made them comical. Everyone had some weird theory or explanation to try to force Bible stories into making sense, but like wild things they squirmed and twisted and defied logic. This battle between bizarre stories and teachers in over their heads bored me: I had questions of my own. I never asked them, until now, because I was afraid. Fear is one of Sunday school's lasting legacies.

I was addicted to horror films ever since "The Crawling Hand" provoked my first hysterical nightmare when I was five years old. I couldn't get enough of them, or of any horror tale. For one thing, "Tales From the Crypt" comics seemed much more likely than Tales from the Bible. Equally bloodthirsty, horror fiction had the advantage of logic, a sense of inevitability and a justice you could feel, while Eden and Joshua and even Jesus seemed contrived, moralistic puppet shows for very dumb children. Yet there was a similarity, one that tied the two together for me, weaving a web between the two.

At 3:00 in the afternoon, "The Aztec Mummy" was as hokey as Jonah. But after dark, the simple story of relentless pursuit by an unconquerable, inescapable, indescribable foe shook me like a doll. Just like God. No matter how good I was all day, how many rules I obeyed, God and the Mummy both lurked by my window just beyond nightfall, each rising from the grave and defying death, each with a curse to fulfill or invoke. Those dry, snapping weeds in the starlight could yield up It or God, watching and waiting. To this day, the nightmares that awaken me, panting and sweating and reaching for the light, are never about punishment or death itself, but of a pursuit I know I will lose, the hand reaching beyond my running, the never sleeping eye.

I have often suspected that my fascination with monster flicks was deeper than the thrill of terror they injected into an otherwise dull, suburban life, more than the surface similarities between formulaic plots and similar biblical narratives. It's like my subconscious was working something out, forcing me to watch these movies in order to seek clues, tricks, tools. It's like something unspeakable had happened to me long before, something so shattering I suppressed even the memory that anything more painful than bee stings or knots on the head had happened to me. But a part of my mind remained vigilant, seeking ways to explain some dreadful deed performed upon my tiny body, searching the world through that magic viewscreen for stories of others who had escaped a monster, tamed the rage and panic now so inexplicable to my waking self, conquered the bloody insides of death to be able to live freely. But because of the question mark at the end of "The Blob," or because I could not find a way to trust a world that had once turned so terribly wrong and unprotecting, I could not fall asleep facing the wall. Until I hit my teens, I had to face the door or I could not sleep. Even the animals I trusted and surrounded myself with at night could not protect my back should Whatever return for more.

Perhaps I devoted myself to piety at such an early age because I thought God might protect me; maybe I just had to know the right prayers or be the right person. Conversely, I just as likely suspected God to be like the perpetrator, only worse, more powerful. In sunlight, piety was a game of rules and asking forgiveness, praying and singing, as easy as watching a movie and peeing during the commercials. Under covers it turned on me, became hiding and fearing unknown, unforgivable rules already broken, listening for the approach that willfully tormented me with its delay. It is now no wonder to me that, upon hitting the bed, I warded off doom by rocking back and forth on my knees, singing beautiful, love-filled Christmas carols into a cocoon around me to stave off God or the Crawling Eye, whichever was there that night. And then collapsing, exhausted and sweaty, pressing my butt against the wall and clutching a stuffed icon of innocence, hoping it all had worked.

I had another secret passion. My earliest erotic memories focused on Hercules films, those dreadful, dubbed Italian styrofoam epics. Hercules was the invincible hero who, laughing at the odds, could escape and defeat any enemy, destroy every trap, kill any monster, defy the gods themselves. His muscled body and bearded good looks, so similar in so many different films, might have been enough for my young queer lust to adhere to. It was his attitude of fighting for right and scoffing danger, his irresistible will to succeed, that proved the more potent aphrodisiac, filling me with hot shame and desire. I could care less if my parents saw me watching "Attack of the Fifty Foot Woman," but I leapt to change channels if Samson was toppling a temple when one of them came in the room. For I feared a double exposure.

In one way I was embarrassed that my thin, flabby body was so unlike Steve Reeves's as to be another life form entirely. This shame hung about me like a spare tire during recess or P.E. at school. In another way, though, my admiration for hulking heroes revealed even to myself an inner paralysis, a sense of utter helplessness with which the ancient monster with no face, no form embraced me. I both desired Herculean strength to fight my own battles, and a big, brave man to rescue me. Long before I discovered the treasures of masturbation, I lay on my stomach before the TV in open-mouthed awe and longing. If I were found enjoying such pleasure, forbidden me by the innate homophobia I breathed daily as well as by a God who forbade even fantasy evasions of just punishments, I would feel humiliated. My fierce vulnerability would be exposed for all to see. Everyone would know I wanted what I could not have, that I needed what no one would offer, that I yearned for both self-sufficient independence and loving dependence. The defiant independence that could not supply dignity for itself and my slavish dependence on an untrustworthy God and unwittingly unprotective parents would be revealed as the paltry tinwhistles they were. And everyone would laugh.

To this day strong men remain powerfully erotic to me, still make me flush with twin embarrassments, make he helplessly seven years old.

As the physical sensations began to center themselves in my groin, my body straining toward puberty, I found that masturbation was wrapped in the Baptist gift paper of guilt and recrimination. Now God had a reason for punishing me. He might forgive my wish to escape him, because he knew I couldn't. Jerking off was open rebellion against his dread rule, it was claiming my body for myself and not offering it as a living sacrifice. It was greedy, ignoble, dirty, selfish. With every stroke I declared myself to be my own. And the fear of discovery perversely spun into pleasure like a drug, quickening the internal thrill in a confusing, maddeningly sensual way.

Because this warfare raged on a wider scale than my childish comprehension could contain, I never really thought about hiding the salty evidence of my sin (stained sheets, handkerchiefs) from my parents; it was all I could do to remember God hated it. I usually ended up on the bathroom floor (the only room that locked), but my need was for private expression of my base, humiliation-filled desires; I didn't care if my parents knew *what* I was doing, so long as they didn't know *why*. What bothered me was The Omniscient One. He didn't like the why or the what. Both were damning: Even if I never masturbated, my petulant desire to be free would enslave me for eternity. If only I could accept slavery to God on earth now, that would save me. I began repenting.

This is how it worked. The urge would come upon me. If I wasn't in class or the mall, I would let it tease me, but I would resist it. My resistance increased its steadily building pressure. Eventually I would give in and run to a private place, chased by furious fantasies of strong men rescuing me, letting me touch them, letting me watch them. Then, after the act, in the breath-catching moments while pleasure drained from my body, I would almost writhe with repentance, pleading with God to save me, take the desire away, forgive my inexcusable weakness.

The sin of homosexuality was incidental: I believed that if I could stop masturbating, I could stop the desire to be free of God. Chaining my body was service to God, and the queer part wouldn't matter. Being queer was minor compared to wanting dignity before God. My energy was not wasted on abstract orientations, but on my body's willful urges. I did sincerely ask God to help me stop. But this is the secret I never even spoke to myself: I did not want to stop. I waited daily for that onset of desire, for the cycle to begin.

Eventually I built the resistance into the fantasy more directly. My attempts to subdue the rising pleasure became erotic foreplay. The object of my desire, some athletic boy from school or Tarzan or someone, would beckon me to give in to his domination. I would try to read the Bible. My will would waver and break under his more powerful command. I would be overcome by his superior attitude and physical beauty. The fantasy man's Herculean will-to-conquer ceased to conquer my inner demons and conquered my piety instead. Giving in became deliciously humiliating.

I eroticized humiliation and helplessness to give them their own power, their own worth. With that feat they no longer terrified me. And the repentance that followed, with its deeper humiliation by a God stronger even than my hero, became sexual as well. God became the ultimate master, and my debasement the highest sacrifice, the noblest piety. It's a baby step from Baptist Sunday School to *Drummer* magazine's "Val Breaks In A Houseslave."

Through high school, I was alone in all of this. All attempts to initiate sex play with other kids floundered. I lusted after athletes at school and fell head over heels in romantic, Tennyson-quoting love with boys who, for me, epitomized strength, beauty, nobility, goodness, and honor. And because these fantasies fell right into the hero-gap of that tortuous time, when my erotic life was so powerfully a part of every hour (ah, youth), the identities I granted these boys became more important to me than any real appreciation of their fragile humanity. They became living archetypes. As with to brutally strong and handsome men, they reduced me to penitent, worshipful attendance. Real love, real sex in a real world have since been infuriatingly compromised by this vortex of adolescent longing that constellated itself into unapproachable ideals of masculine excellence.

But they saved my life and sanity, in literal ways: My dry, daytime fantasies drove back the tide of depression and stormy self-contempt that roared loudly in my ears. These daydreams of romantic rescue from despair, in which the boys inevitably offered me their love like a rose, instilled a physical hope I could feel and cry over. And record in atrocious verse.

Which isn't to say I turned my back on Christianity. Being an earnest child, I wanted Christianity to make sense as much as my mentally gymnastic Sunday School teachers did. I wanted it to be a religion of joy and light and salvation. I tried to pay attention no matter how tiresome church services became, I prayed daily (separate from my sexual prayers) to a God I imagined to be gentle and good. I tried not to swear or lie quite so much. I wanted God not just to save me—or spare me—but to like me. And while I obediently loved God, I truly wanted to like God, and sought out meditatively likable aspects of him. Sometimes I found them in Jesus, but Jesus was never more than a salvific functionary for me. It was God the Great and Terrible, behind his savage curtain of billowing fire, whom I sought to see as really a kindly old man, bluff and bluster hiding a caring heart.

My two lives of secret sexual tension and resolution and extroverted intellectual investigation and playfulness mirrored God's schizophrenic aspect so like two-faced Janus or those statues of beneficent Ganesa with a glowering demon head on the backside of the kindly elephantine face. And I somehow carved out time to be a child from the glacier of seriousness that crowded my life. Growing in that time was the awareness of having an alternative vision of things as a result of these two lives. I not only walked with a natural, unaffected swish from an early age (in which I take pride) but I seemed to want to play different games than other children, make up new ones, combine girl and boy games into one. I sang and danced my way dramatically through life, wrote little screenplays and cast impromptu neighborhood dramas. I saw no problem between having GI Joe drop by Barbie's Dreamhouse for tea. (I also liked to stripsearch Joe, but always in private.) Somewhere along the line I learned that even this creativity was dangerous, that any distinguishing feature I showed other children than the two "legitimate" choices of sports or brains would not just move me outside the popularity circle, but into the outland of nerd-dom. (Brains themselves were partially suspect, but I let everyone copy my homework, so I was "cool." I considered it communist subversion.) I had no intention of letting my personal uniqueness make me a nerd, the butt of jokes and pranks. I suppressed and blunted my personality in order to gain acceptance that meant safety from physical abuse.

Between my two lives, I learned what Life was while other kids were busy living it: Life is where you got caught. And "truth" was the biggest trap of all: Only heroic strength and beauty could set you free.

Of course this was parallel to repressing my sexuality before God, and eventually I sank into a suicidal depression that lasted most of my teenage years. When the throes of adolescence gelled into a firmer identity and sense of self, I began to release my pent-up creations, and long-simmering anger. And I challenged God's heterosexist demands on my life.

It was during this time that I found Lutheranism. It was through Campus Ministry at college, so for the first three years I met very few blond, lutefisk-toting, garden variety "cultural" Lutherans. I received pure Luther, scrutinized by idealistic youths who also sought a loving, good God. And in Luther's thought, gay people cannot be separated from others. In the lyrical liturgy and *sturm und drang* hymnody I found a God who didn't "save" me because it was in his job description (like the Baptists' Old Man Grumpus) but because, rather like the Academy and Sally Field, he liked me, he really liked me. Finally, I thought, a God I could like. This God offered promises of a full life and freedom from oppression (or, at least, oppression's deleterious effects) instead of threats and cudgels about my ears. And there began another long, winding journey.

"We weren't lovers/just brave strangers/as we fought and we tumbled through the night," Bob Seger sings as if summing up my relationship with God during these years. As a Baptist, in spite of God's glowering threats, I had felt an intimacy with God. No doubt an intimacy forged in the furnace of a spiritual Hellfire Club, but a closeness nonetheless. As a Lutheran, I wrestled God like Jacob, my biblical namesake, for top. Moments of anger and doubt were joined with rapturous ecstasy, feeling God's caressing hand. Questions that had been building up ever since childhood about the logical gaps in Salvation History kept popping up, and they were welcome now. (What did happen to people before there was Jesus? Who did Cain marry? Why did Paul get to write the New Testament and Peter get to run the church for eternity? Did Paul know he was writing the Bible? There seemed to be more Assumptions here than just Mary's.) With Lutheran scholarship, I was able for a time to satiate my questions. There seemed to be answers for everything. And being a restless, flaming queen, I boldly went to seminary to search out more answers.

Seminary in Berkeley, California, is truly a many-splendored thing. Given no center other than Liberal Political Orthodoxy, life in the People's

Republic becomes a movable feast of questions, answers and koans. My questions, and Christianity's answers, moved deeper than "Do we go straight to heaven like in 'Brainstorm' or do we wait like in 'Our Town?'"

I began to question why God offered so little direct support of me in my teenage struggle for survival other than being the one taking the credit for keeping the gun out of my mouth. (I often cited as an article of faith that God kept me from committing suicide: That protection was at the heart of my "gay theology.") I began to question the constant harping on sin and forgiveness, and the crippling moral effects of "Only God is Good" theology. With a measure of desperation, I believed the answers, and the theology, more rashly than before.

At first the idea that "God is suffering with the oppressed" was comforting (as compared to God's ignoring it), but after a while I started to wonder why God, Creator of the Rolling Spheres Ineffably Sublime, was content to sit and suffer with me? I wasn't content to do it: I wanted suffering to stop, and was working toward it. Why couldn't God do anything? God, after all, was infinitely greater than I, who never even created a single loving sphere, and who was incredibly mundane.

We are taught that the Bible proposes a God active in history, hence the Incarnation, but why isn't God active in *my* history? I took the fury in the Psalms seriously, and began to wonder if their true author eventually became an atheist, thus their ascription to David and Solomon, et al. God's answer to Job's similar questions, "I'm bigger and busier than you, so shut up," began to seem more and more like a line.

But, trooper that I was, I found amid the flotsam and jetsam of Christian tradition a few boards and splinters with which to build a theology in which I could live. I found that I had less and less in common with other people who called themselves "Christians." And, out of my years of steady activism and agitation, an opportunity to act in a big way opened like a divine invitation.

My last year at seminary was bisected by the gay march on Washington. Many of my gay Lutheran classmates went, a couple of us missing our certification interviews to do so. (Certification is the first step in the ordination process.) While at the march, I made the decision to transfer into the Universal Fellowship of Metropolitan Community Churches; reading Malcolm X at the same time, with his hard line about blacks teaching in white colleges when the community needs them, inspired me as well. Jeff Johnson, Joel Workin and I were going up for certification as candidates for ordination in December of 1987, and we argued long and hard for the best way to strike a political blow for civilization. Our friend and advisor, Greg Egertson, would follow us the next year and so was left out of the official proceedings that followed, but was profoundly influential. It was a marvelous, heady time for us all.

Even though I was leaving the church, I wanted two things: I wanted the certification I had worked for and deserved (it would serve me also in the MCC) and I wanted to give the church a hard time. For in spite of Luther's remarkably inclusive theology, the Lutheran churches in the United States remain impervious to gay truths and gay demands. Like Sunday School, it stands against such logic. Joel, Jeff and I decided to come out to our certification committees, and let it be known we wanted to be certified as openly gay candidates for ordination. We were already out on campus, but we wanted to make sure they knew what they were doing. We were all certified as openly gay men, and none of us were asked to pledge an oath of life-long celibacy.

There were many political dynamics undergirding that situation, including a huge, national church merger occurring at the same time. The details are unimportant: As Jean Brodie says, "For those who like that sort of thing, that is the sort of thing they like," and are duly recorded elsewhere. The main battle assumed the following shape.

We sent out a press release, via Lutherans Concerned/San Francisco (the Lutheran gay caucus), that three openly gay men were certified as candidates for ordination in the Evangelical Lutheran Church of America (ELCA). The press was slow to pick it up: The ELCA's organ, The Lutheran, to whom the story was leaked early, continued to delay publication. When the story hit the AP wire and was carried around the country near the end of February, 1988, the ground shook around campus. In the press deluge that followed (replete with radio interviews and even a mention on CNN), the church responded with all the weight and pomposity it could muster.

The bishops called a meeting to deal with us, sending representatives from Chicago. On March 24, 1988, the Berkeley Three (as we had been dubbed) met with two bishops and two church hierarchs in the Synod offices in Oakland. At that point we were told that the purpose of the meeting was not to work out our differences, as they had previously informed us by letter. The church had only two things on their minds: Were we fucking now, and did we ever intend to fuck again in our lives. That was all.

Lambs to the slaughter, we had waved aside advice to have either a lawyer or a tape recorder present. The hierarchs, of course, didn't say "fucking"—they said "practicing." We asked them to define that: Does holding hands count? Our opponents refused to define their euphemism, allowing its vagueness to waver like a lasso, ready to be pulled tight around us whenever they chose. The bishops refused to meet us on what we considered equal terms at all, or consider our issues or gifts or solutions. As coldly as Panzer tanks they cut down our responses and ignored our questions. Then we were each brought before the committee individually.

I had not been expecting such an ambush. Stupidly, I had expected the church to deal honorably and fairly with us according to its stated policies and guidelines (none of which called for celibacy for anyone). We were qualified candidates whom qualified church representatives had found acceptable by church standards, and even if we did make the general public aware of the church's decision to certify us, we had informed the Bay Area bishop prior to sending out the release. But instead of calm, rational interaction, our concerns were met with base intimidation and bare-fisted insults. The eventual outcome of that four-hour afternoon inquisition was that no bishop would recommend us for ordination in the ELCA: We were qualified, but no one would employ us.

Although I had committed to leave the church, the shadowy trenches of the bishops' guerrilla tactics had shell-shocked me. My firm resolve dissolved and I was suddenly moving to a different rhythm of priorities, one that whispered "stay alive." My world tilted: Beset literally on all sides by hostile men with enormous power, alarms were ringing in my head. The personal attack was as extreme as any gay-bashing I've experienced. Their faces and voices were open sewers of hatred. I was only glad to leave without having cried for them.

The next day I did cry. Stepping out of the shower, I was suddenly wracked with sobs, and sat weeping on the toilet lid for half an hour. In my "History of Black Religious Thought" class later that morning we discussed the riots and lynchings of the turn of this century. The stories rang true, and I embarrassedly struggled for composure with everyone in class looking at me strangely. For the next few weeks I would be overcome with paranoia, I jumped when anyone touched me unexpectedly, had fits in which I locked all the windows and doors and sat in the middle of the floor. Policemen made me flinch.

Meanwhile I graduated. Straight students flooded the ceremony with large pink triangles in support of us. I moved to Los Angeles and began working in the MCC. On the tails of my inquisition, it was some months before I could enter a church without shaking, but I forged on with the procedures set before me. And when they were sure the atmosphere was free of too many attackers, my questions poked their little heads out again.

With careful study and deliberation, listening to my heart, I found it harder and harder to align myself with Christian traditions. I found it trickier to justify the patriarchal oppression to which the Bible witnesses, harder to find any true revelation of a trustworthy and honorable God amid the cruelty and waste of the conquest of Canaan. The interminable prophecies against idolatry began to sound provincial, demeaning, hollow facades fronting a systematic suppression of women. I couldn't bear a God so entirely male, and yet so entirely passive as to allow so much wrong to be committed on God's behalf. I grew tired of the crucified God who focuses us on death, whose own resurrection is an academic fact bearing no fruit in my bruised flesh. My own rape under the grunting hands of church officials and the deep depression that followed may have pushed it all to the fore, but the questions of my childhood retain their own power: Where do I find my dignity? Where does God respect my worth? Where, in this desolate land of material wealth, is God anything more than a moral burr under the saddle of an exhausted horse? And haven't I been through enough that I don't need God's comfort, but God's protection? Hasn't everyone?

Were I to meet God today, I would rise to meet God. I would ask God to explain how it is that God did not stop the person who abused me so severely that I still cannot remember what happened, and ask why I have had to waste so much time in pursuing a ghost I cannot catch. My phantom catches me at odd moments during sex or conversation, filling my body with tight fear and my mind with confused apprehension. Where is God in that?

When God answered that satisfactorily, I would ask God how it is that so many helpless people are abused by bigger, stronger, more devious people. And when God has answered that, I would ask God to explain why children die. And when God explained that, I would ask God to explain disease, deformations, sudden deaths. And when God explained that, I would ask God to explain AIDS.

And when God offers me an answer to AIDS that I can rest with, I will ask God about other plagues, and other epidemics. And when God tells me why they happen, I will ask about tyranny and slavery, and why they exist. When God tells me that, I will ask about hunger. When God tells me all about hunger, I will ask God about famines, and droughts, and pestilence. And when God answers me that, I will ask why people are oppressed by gender, by race, by class, by idiocy, by greed, by fear. And when God is able to come up with something that will make sense of all that, I will simply ask God, "Why?"

And when God tells me "why," I will weep. I will gently fall to the earth and weep. And if God can respond to my weeping with humility, and can preserve my precious dignity which I have fought every day of my life to shield like a jewel, then I will call that being God. If God cannot respond to that, in a way that is unimaginably, immediately true, then that thing is an imposter, full of lies and clotted with blood. It will not be the god I seek. I will have to search for another.

I cannot say what sort of god I believe exists, but I no longer believe in any God any tradition has offered me. And I am offended at the humiliation which the majority of "gods" inflict on people who have a hard enough time as it is. I suspect the god I seek is intangible, barely palpable, throbbing under the flesh, in trees, under the sea. But if I find a god in this world, it must be worthy of my love, for I will accept nothing less from any god.

For now, I am spending my time on myself and on those on love. I have hard questions to ask myself as well: It's not like I'm on vacation. Where do I find sexual healing, that will allow me the freedom of sexual interactions without the little bombshells of smoldering memories that literally throw me out of bed when a "hot spot" is unknowingly touched? What do I do with the fears that continue to follow me: How do I turn Harpies into Eumenides? In a life whose boundaries were systematically smashed, where do I learn safe ways to enjoy what is erotic to me, and eroticize what has become dull with health? I am sensitive to the criticism launched against the S/M community which alleges that all S/M is rooted in abuse, and I support Scott Tucker's and others' articulate defenses of S/M practice; I do not want to add my own stories of abuse to the general criticism. Yet how do I preserve what is healthy and enjoyable, and not indulge those neuroses that further entrap my spirit in the lie of helplessness? Particularly, how do I do this when feeling helpless? These are some questions I have for myself, and for my community. And if there is a god with any answers worthy of questions, s/he may answer as well.

Now it is clearer than it was then. Then the monsters who pursued me under the flannel and into my nightmares were everywhere, taking anyone's face. Growing up as isolated gay and lesbian people, we often have to test the people we most love and trust to see if their faces will suddenly distort with monstrous hatred; it's not knowing who our real enemies are that wears us down. Coming out is the process whereby we sort out who's who, gaining some measure of control over the random give and take (and often, take and take and take) of life. But one monster I had to stalk was the hardest one of all. Not the nameless one who abused me (his face remains hidden), nor the individuals who, out of their own pain, confusion or rage, injured me or those I loved. There's miles of forgiveness for them. The one monster most heart-breaking to face has been the one offering salvation himself, the one I most needed saving from. That monster is a God who pits my sense of self against my mind, my reason, my body, my perceptions. Like a blood-engorged spider, that creature created lose-lose situations wherein I had to choose between myself or God's love, where happiness in this world had to be traded against joy in another, and who prompted adults to terrorize children with tales flowing with gore, death and guilt.

In driving that God from the new Eden of my world, I have claimed my body and my world for a god beyond the petty trivialities of saying one particular name or praying one particular prayer. And if that god is no less than myself and no greater than the vast expanse of human passion and hope from all time to all time, then it is yet an honorable god. And the story of such a god will truly be a tale worth telling.

James Lancaster was born in the early sixties, and protected from them by a Southern Baptist home. In the second grade, his teacher had to restrain him from kissing other boys. He became Lutheran in college, active in campus ministry and, to the consternation of many, the Gay and Lesbian Student Union. He had always wanted to be an actor but went to seminary instead. He achieved notoriety when, in the spring of 1988, he and two other seminarians sent out a press release that they had been certified for ordination in the newly merged Evangelical Lutheran Church in America as openly gay candidates. In the furor that followed, they were summarily barred from employment in the church. James now makes his home in Los Angeles, where he is writing a novel. He has no pets.

DAVE JOHNSON

Dancing in the Arms
of the Mystery

S ometimes I almost remember the beginning, and before the beginning. It comes as a flash, a fragment. I see images: a long journey, an absolute serenity, a light, an option, a falling into the light. Then it seems a dream, but like all dreams more real in the backward blink of an eye than waking itself. There brushes against the edges of my being a feeling that if I could just pierce the teasing veil, I would remember. I would understand. I would open my eyes beyond my eyes and see.

It haunts me. Perfectly benevolent. Patient as eternity. The mystery.

In the shining cultures the white man hounded from this land, the name for God is Great Mystery. In the dominant culture's sad quest for a neatly ordered world, they have lost that level of respect for God. They think they have figured it all out, abandoning the humble search that is the root of spiritual practice. Like all attempts at confining reality with the intellect, the result is all about them, and not about God at all.

God is not confined. How easily we forget that it is God, and not us, who chooses what God is. It cannot be otherwise. And God chooses the Mystery.

The hardest thing any parent must do is hold back. The loving parent knows that to love is to allow personhood to grow; to provide parameters, but not formulas; to create choices, but not to make them; to guide, but not to manipulate; to withhold wisdom, so that the child might be born into wisdom through experience. So it must be with God. And thus the Mystery.

As a child I remember gradually awakening into this journey in wonder and great surprise. My first actual, literal memory here is simple, celluloid. I am walking down Laurel Avenue, near what is now a very gay part of Los Angeles, California. My grandmother is there. I am living, reacting, speaking, utterly without hesitation, perhaps for the last time. I am just shy of two years old.

I have a strange sense that I remembered more then; that I was still connected somehow to where I had just come from, but had to abandon that secret knowledge to move fully into the world. It was as if a door was closing behind me. One day I will pass through that door again, and know.

In the world I found great wonder and terrible violence. Unbeknownst to me I had walked into a complex web of expectations which had nothing to do with me. I had entered the lives of two talented and volatile people. In creating a family, they were determined to find the control—and therefore safety—ripped away from them on their separate paths long before.

My father was an orphan from a small town in rural Pennsylvania. From his earliest days there had been a terrible war between the gentle and caring man born in him, and the brutality all around him in which he had to find a home. By the time I came along, he had emerged from that battleground an actor—and an alcoholic. Thus did the spark and the terror merge.

My mother was a brilliant woman, in an age that did not allow her to exist. Her need for control was desperate; her temper violent and unpredictable, even to her.

When I came, they held for me a detailed script, for which I was badly miscast.

There was violence and there was drinking. There was terror and confusion. Worst of all, there was the impossible division from self that comes when people speak pretty words and do brutal things in the dark; when the world becomes insane and there is nothing left but to flee and hide.

I remember when it happened to me. When I would cry, and my father was not around, my mother would drag me to the sink and hold my head under water to make me stop. The memory has no sound. I remember flying through the air. I remember the pale porcelain sink coming nearer, the drain like a dreadful empty eye, now in a kind of slow motion.

The free engagement with the world was over. I must have longed to return from whence I had come. But the door had closed. There could be no return. The breath of the Mystery had borne away the memory of the veil just crossed.

And so I found another way to leave. There came a kind of void, a waking oblivion, a complete disengagement, especially from my own self. A terrible blankness in which I dared not express, and learned to control. Interaction was now about strategy, reaction, defense. I learned to do what would make them stop. And I began to assume terrible lies about myself.

It must have pained God to hold back in those first years; but God, like a parent, cannot walk the child's path. Instead, God relentlessly creates possibilities, new doors. We enter them or not, and do what we will on the journey, for as long as it takes. That is the way of the parent, and the point of the journey.

The gentle doors in my path saved my life. When the violence at home shut me down, the love of my grandparents brought me back. Here were two people who seemed to notice who I was, and who were glad to see me. In honoring me as exactly who I was, in celebrating me without strings, they helped me to honor and celebrate myself. They were my mirrors and my witnesses. At home, I was living entirely in relation to what other people might do or expect; with them I was able to simply be.

In this way, I learned to come into the world when I felt it was safe, and to detach the rest of the time. The price of this lesson was high. The strain, the division of the world into us and them, into safe and unsafe places, was becoming a dangerous habit—one that has pursued and seduced me all my life, and seduces my tribe still.

Deep within me there was my own special magic, fighting to get free. There was a spirit, a seed, a vision. Something that still knew. Something that remained innocent of the world and its madness. The relentless center of light, determined to grow. The portal of the Mystery in my heart, the well-spring of my new and unique contribution to it.

It needed to come alive, and not just in the company of my grandparents. I needed a way to live it.

One day a cat wandered into our yard. I was about four years old. I believe it was the first time I had ever seen a cat in my life. The bonding was instant, like only a child bonds. My shining center leaped like a fearless dancer into the arms of obvious likeness. In that cat's eyes, the Mystery opened another door. The cat's love was like the love of God, was the love of God; clear, direct, without thought, as if no other possibility made sense.

I made up a world populated entirely by cats, and me, called Cats Town. I played there, generally alone, throughout my childhood.

Thus in the cradle of imagination was my vision kept alive through all the madness that had nothing to do with me. I can still see the boy that I was then—delightful in his innocence, magnificent in his simple courage; he knows nothing else. He is the hero of my life. He survives, and teaches me still.

There was always something about my magic that was quite different from the other boys around me. I remember my father's friends calling me "Russell's faggot son." I love to watch old movies of myself, dancing and waving my arms in the air, nellie as hell, and not caring—not even knowing, unable to conceive that my behavior was other than beautiful, other than simply me. Innocent still of the killing requirements of manhood, I just danced. And already there was in my flesh, in my eyes, in charged games in secret bushes, the hint of the magical queer bonding, the astonishing and simple bridge, the moment when the walls and the terror melted and two boys became one, cheating the high priests of their sacrifice.

So much was coming forth; so much dangerous, impossible, full of passion and wonder. As I grew older I began to create strategies to protect myself. School had begun, and more and more of my time was engaged in dealing with the outside world. Rules were invented, assumptions were made, that mirrored the insanity that provoked them. I became aloof and withdrawn, with a caution in my eyes that should not have haunted them so young. I came to believe my parents' public display of me as a boy wonder, and thus honed my shining young intellect into the weapon of arrogance to maintain the distance and survive.

I learned to separate entirely from the world, to live inside myself, to observe, calculate, anticipate, and respond as necessary.

Except in Cats Town. Except in the play worlds. There I ran free, and thus am alive.

I was not a popular child. I was, after all, both the smart kid and the sissy; the one who got the best grades and the last one picked on the baseball team. This combination, combined with the choice of conceit as a defense, was not a success. I see myself then, striking back with arrogance that masked horrible self-doubt and sarcasm that shielded violent pain. I taste the tears I was afraid to cry to anyone. I remember holding the tears close inside, deep in my chest, as if I feared that losing them would blast me down a slippery careening slope, out of the pale starving safety of my isolation, into the world of them.

Yet in glimpses and moments it would still come, a connection, a peace, a simple grace. The Mystery and the magic grew together at the center of my being, partners in the nurturing soil of my sprouting personhood. I remember I was always questioning, always exploring. Sheltered, deep inside, the heart of me still grew, parallel to the act outside and having nothing to do with it, waiting in secret to emerge.

And I know now that God had never left me. I always felt the presence; felt it at so basic a level that I did not know I felt it.

But I could not know God by name.

For the dominant culture all around me had honed its collective intellect into a weapon, too. They had used that magnificent tool to create miracles, and had puffed themselves up beyond remembrance of their gentle partner in the miracles. They had fallen into the seductive illusion of order that is the price of reliance on the mind only. They had come to fear all that they could not control. Above all, they had to contain and imprison God.

To do this they had invented dogma and religion. They had built great steel boxes of words to trap God and then lived in them.

My mother made her choice of boxes when I was three years old. She became a Christian Scientist.

Of all the God boxes I have explored in my life since, Christian Science seems a peculiarly modern one, a kind of ultimate tyranny of the intellect over any trace of wonder, or its essential partner, doubt. In Christian Science, it is all figured out. One merely needs to think properly, and all problems are solved. Things like sickness and death—indeed the body and all matter—are simply "not real," a truly incredible oxymoron of denial that could only be achieved by departing the world and living among the neurons.

Trained as I was that being the best at everything was both my calling and the price of survival, I became the best little Christian Scientist there was. I knew I could trust my intellect; to give it such absolute power made me feel primally safe. But I could not know God by name, the God who now desired an open and intimate relationship with me as I matured. In the God box we may only relate to our model of God, which blinds us to God's simple and obvious embrace.

Yet the grace and creativity of God found these walls of religion no limitation at all. Sometimes through the church, often in spite of it, the love and guidance were always there, and my wonder and magic continued to grow.

I remember there often being a great joy in living largely inside myself. I remember the worlds of imagination I fled to; I spent marvelously happy times there.

But I could not stay there forever. I had to find a way to bond genuinely and powerfully to others, in a world in which I had so far found ridicule, envy, and only the briefest of respite with a few people.

For that problem, the Mystery and the magic had a powerful and elegant solution.

I had always wanted to play with and touch the other boys, for as long as I can remember. As early as four or five years old there were games, the moments of charged curiosity. I sought a bridge, a bonding. I knew it was there. I felt drawn to it, magnetized, electric all over at the thought.

Through a lot of trial and error with other boys, and the timid, eloquent teaching of an older man, the spark of gay tribal sex play came into my life. What a gift! What a blessing, that I discovered sex before I was imprisoned by the lies; that I learned sex was wonderful, innocent, spectacular, before anyone had a chance to tell me it was shameful and dirty.

And what a supreme irony that this culture, which worships violence, accepts injustice, and normalizes the most terrible suffering, would castigate that older man as the lowest thing on earth. I have not seen him in twenty years. If I met him tomorrow, I would embrace him, and kiss him, and thank him.

As the wonderful secret sex play with the boys grew, I found myself in the bizarre position of being ridiculed and abused by these boys in public, while having sex with practically all of them in private.

This was, of course, the root of the violent patterns all the brothers of my tribe carry: the double life, the gut-biting viper of self-contempt, the growing irrelevance of trust, the descent into the pit of the angry victim.

But it taught me a brilliant lesson as well. Turned upside down, viewed from a different angle, this dreadful duality also showed me that behind every man's trained brutality, beneath and beyond every false and sickening movie of manhood projected icily on a hardened face, there lies the boy— waiting in secret, wide-eyed, innocent, ready to play, able to leap the fatal chasm with ease and banish the pale granite prison with his gentle touch.

Thus it was that the vision reached beyond my own heart only and became a vision for the tribe.

My adolescence was savaged and robbed by the ugly war that every queer boy knows: the searing battle between who you are and what the voices inside tell you that means. I was discovering my community; it was the early 1970s, and there was the original Metropolitan Community Church, the old Gay Center in the rickety house on Wilshire Boulevard, the gay-ins in Griffith Park. I had found my tribe.

And yet voices not mine continued to slash and burn at the very guts of my being, and rip me away from connection and peace. They told me I was not who I was, that I could never bond with the others like me.

This desperate and unwinnable holocaust inside ended, as it always ends, with a truce—a truce of denial, cynicism, buried rage turned inward, behavior without heart, a cruel parody of the tribal spark played on empty pastel stages, shrouded in utter worthlessness.

I became the modern gay man.

In this post-war world there was no room for faith. Given a choice between my religion and my survival, I had chosen the latter. And I know now that God understood perfectly.

I quickly drew to myself the sad buttresses of the life spent running from pain. The descent into drinking and drugs was quick and inevitable.

Yet even there, there was both the hungry pit and the lingering, pulsing spark. Most of my daily drug use was about the burial of pain, but much was amazing exploration, growth, emergence. Drugs had become the new Cats Town. Self-preservation and self-destruction became the parallel solutions, the chaff and the wheat, waiting, teetering, as the harvest grew near.

Romance in those days was painful and disappointing. Like all gay men,

I so feared who I really was that I could not conceive of creating it in my life. I sought instead to find again the terrible patterns of my unresolved past: the man who could not love me, the flashes of comfort with a few safe people, the use of sex as a brief and devious bonding snatched from those who cared nothing for me. These patterns and nightmares I would relive, and do it right this time, and fix it. My hand could not reach freely forth; it was too busy clutching the script under my arm.

But God never gave up, because God does not know how to give up, and cannot imagine why anyone else does. On a drunk and vacant night, in the barstool dark where there are no faces, dressed in the mortal remains of several dead cows, Lonnie Richards appeared in my life.

I fell in love quickly, which in those days meant I was sure I had found the perfect rewrite of the past, and would clutch it at all costs. It was, in fact, an old pattern that brought me to the table with Lonnie. Most of my childhood had been spent careening back and forth between desperate attempts to gain my father's love, and retreat to the safety of my grandmother's indulgence. My grandmother was a bright and charming person with a soothing Texas accent, and so was Lonnie.

But God can be very sneaky when She has to be. The pattern was a ruse. The spark reached its once-withered hand up from its starved hiding place and filled my fingers again. It began first as a glow, a simple warmth unlike any other. And then, across the years of terror, the child in me leapt the dreadful wall, incredibly, with the simple elegance of a dove in unhurried flight. Before I knew it, I was in an entirely new world: a real relationship, with a man I loved completely.

Slowly we built together a life of strange balance and carefully controlled ecstasy. I had never been happier in my life. We grew into a wonderful kind of contentment I had never known before. And when the pain and the memories got too close, there was my old friend the bottle, who demanded greater and greater doses of worship as the price of precarious stability.

Then there stole into our house the vicious plunderer, the horror that drains our bodies of life bit by torturous bit and enters into laughing alliance with the old voices of self-hate, blaming us for its violence on the way out, just for spite. Lonnie was diagnosed with AIDS.

His death was an endless screaming nightmare, a tunnel whose suffocating walls dripped acid, a pain, at last, I could not drink away. The balance shattered forever. Finally the price of retreat was death itself. I reached that dizzying moment every alcoholic faces at the edge of the cliff: the moment where it all ends, and the choice is to stop or die.

In the dazed morning after there was only one way to survive, and that was to give up. To stop trying to hold it together. To embrace the inevitability of total surrender. Standing on the edge of a chasm like so many I had known—the pale porcelain sink of infancy, the lying pit of vipers tearing at my self-worth in adolescence—I finally, simply let go.

And there to catch me, laughing and weeping for joy, was the God I had cynically abandoned, but who had never for a moment abandoned me.

At first, the rhetoric in recovery about a "Higher Power" was frightening and distancing. I felt the tentacles of the religious dictatorship of my youth crawling around inside of me. It was a sickening and familiar feeling; I felt for a moment as though I was going to have to lose the wonder of my identity, my queerness, in order to live.

This moment of panic came from the terrible and classic absurdity that pervades most religious training, which asserts that God is into extortion— that God blesses you for doing what God wants, and hurts you if you do not.

By the grace of God I soon awakened to a simpler truth: that God loves unconditionally, that God is unconditional love itself. And I began to believe it only because it began to work for me. Everywhere the right person was there at the right time. I felt surrounded, enveloped. I had a sense of vast forces mobilized, of rich energies cascading over me as a soothing balm and a shocking life preserver.

Given the pain in my life I had always thought that God must be awfully subtle; quickly in recovery I realized that I had been awfully dense. I began to see that the same power that rallied to my rescue now had been there all along: in the love of my grandmother, in the eyes of the cat in the back yard, in Lonnie's gentle face emerging from the cold, strangling dark, always working, always right on time.

And now the harvest is come. Now the chaff is cast to the winds by the relentless tools thrust in my hand, the doors ever opened: a wonderful therapist, workshops, meetings, new friends, a nurturing church community. Now the plan comes clearer. Now the power leads, and I give my hand freely.

And at long last, set free of the rules and chains that drowned the magic so long in scotch and desperate orgasmic parody, I become what I had always dreamed of while falling off barstools. I find the work, the movement. I contribute to the liberation of my tribe. I step into leadership and launch a power I have held and hidden for years on the bloody waters of these times.

Finally I know how to trust. At last I know how to be wrong and not die of it. The tyrant intellect is surrendered to the questing boy, full of the old wonder, open to God's self-definition and co-creation with and through God's children.

It was always an extraordinary journey; now my eyes are open on the road. That's a good thing. You have fewer accidents that way. I am taking it all in, and learning, and celebrating, and hurting, and not running away.

There have been, and will be, times of sheer terror on this path. But the road is decorated with freshness and rewards far beyond the exile dreams of beer haze and spunk on the floor.

I look forward now to the future. Even death is no longer fearsome. I cannot imagine that the power now holding my hand would have anything but wonderful plans beyond that last margin of surrender, that final door, that simple reconnection to the Mystery.

I look forward, and these things I know: that there is a loving God, a vast power far smarter than I am, which continually creates new possibilities in my life, which I may accept or not, for as long as it takes; that that energy is not only loving, but is love itself, and is profoundly simple, and contains no element that is not love; that surrender to that power not only takes not one speck away from one's own self, but is the completion of one's own self, the obvious partner in rich and expanding identity; that walking the path willingly showers one's life with blessings beyond one's dreams; that God has no agenda of punishment, but only of reconciliation, and that horrors spoken to the contrary are figments of the fevered and desperate imagination of egos for whom absolute control is the prerequisite of imagined safety; that on the journey we may turn and face where we wish but we are always dancing our lives in the arms of the Mystery, where comfort, safety and guidance are ever there for the asking; that we often turn from this inexhaustible nurturing because we cannot trust and therefore do not like the answer because it is not ours; that we lesbian and gay people are a special delight in the eyes of God, who laughs at us when we play with each other and weeps for joy when we find love in the midst of the horror; that my relationship to God and yours are each direct, nurturing, and unique, requiring—indeed admitting—no intermediaries; that the relationship calls us to action in the face of the terror of these times, to "do justice, and to love mercy, and to walk humbly with our God"; that the boundless power of love which God represents in this world will ultimately triumph, because it is the only real power, and because the alternative is absurd and contains no possible future.

And I know something else as well. I look into the eyes of the man I love. I feel the wonder of the relationship in my life that is the most beautiful gift of all. We are both struggling with HIV. I see the simple courage, the serenity, the rich and passionate love. I feel these things, and I understand. I know that the shining heart of my lesbian and gay tribe is one more door, one more brilliant piece of the relentless plan for the healing of this world. I am very proud. And I am at peace.

Dave Johnson became the first executive director of Being Alive/ People with AIDS Action Coalition in L.A. and later was named AIDS coordinator for the City of Los Angeles by Mayor Tom Bradley. Recently he left that position to become a full-time writer and activist.

In his late teens he became intensely involved in the emerging gay liberation movement and, in 1973, assumed leadership of the UCLA Gay Students Union. Afterward, in the late '70s, he pursued a successful career in data processing and business management. After he was diagnosed with AIDS-related complex (ARC), he decided to leave the private sector and return to community involvement.

He lists his favorite things as "heated debate, dazzling conversation, Monteverdi, Monet, Mahler, Vivaldi, Telemann, David Bowie, Phillip Glass, Walt Whitman, Pat Parker, politics, religion, roses, scruffy men in leather, camping, traveling, the beach, shopping, laughter, Godzilla movies, and being in love with Ric."

ROBERT W. GUNN
Reclaiming the Lost Self

My sexuality and spirituality have always been closely allied in my life, bound together around the poles of ecstasy and shame. They also constitute my earliest memories: By the age of four, I had been indelibly impressed by the image of my cousin's body beside me in bed and the strange but powerful attraction to him I felt; and I had been enthralled by the power of my grandfather's Southern Methodist preaching and singing and wanted to share it.

Just before I turned ten, I had a conversion experience in which I went down to the altar in expulsive, sobbing tears, to surrender my life to Christ. I was filled with a conviction of God's love for me and my unworthiness of it. The ability to surrender, to go down and publicly acknowledge my sinfulness, and thereby be open to grace, was itself an act of grace. God only knows how we sometimes can let it in, and sometimes shut the door.

That experience, and the conviction it brought of God's unconditional love, remained a pivotal experience of my life, a divining rod by which all other events and claims were to be evaluated.

After my conversion, the most ecstatic experiences I had were in my teens when swimming naked with fellow Boy Scouts in the river under moonlight, then getting together in tents afterward. It always seemed to me that those experiences meant more to me than the other guys, so, heavy with guilt and shame, I tried to put them out of my mind. I remember coming home after one such excursion and wondering if somehow my mother could tell what had happened by the khaki shorts I was wearing. Nothing had happened in them or with them, but they were sexy as hell, so I felt guilty about it.

By the age of fourteen, when it became clear that there was no place for my real sexual interests in the world, the polarity between sexuality and spirituality became a chasm which I couldn't imagine being bridged, especially by God. My sexual self became filled with shame and so I stored it away; my persona, which was all that was good, acceptable and rewarded in the world, contained my spirituality. Thus there was no room in my theology or spiritual practice for sex, except as a cause of remorse, confession and self-hate. I became adept at dividing my thought and feelings and words between what was spontaneous and shameful and therefore to be suppressed, and what was acceptable in society. While thus killing my self slowly on the inside, I was successful by conforming on the outside.

The church, whose mandate is the saving of souls, was united with society in condemning mine. If God is the one you turn to when everyone else lets you down, what do you do when you're told that, on this issue, not even God is there for you? What kind of spirituality can you have when your core self is buried in shame? The very tools by which you learn to live in the world and survive in such a situation (denial, repression, sublimation, etc.) are barriers to the experience of grace, because the heart from which all feelings flow has already been condemned for its longings. I managed the conflict by making major splits in my personality, separating body from mind; good-me from bad-me; sex from intimacy; the open, personable me from the secret, shame-filled, sexual me; and of course, God from sex.

There is an essential connection between sexuality and spirituality and the intersection is the self. If faith claims I'm loved unconditionally, "just as I am," and that the One who loves me is one "unto whom all hearts are open, all desires known, and from whom no secrets are hid" (Methodist Collect), then there is an intimate connection between my sexuality, my natural spontaneous loving movements, and my spirituality, which is the point of contact with the Great Lover. But under conditions of homophobia in the church and society, what should be an embracing polarity between sexuality and spirituality becomes a split in which both energies are buried by shame. There can be no vital spirituality when the core sexual self is in shame. But in college and seminary in the '60s, I understood nothing of this.

In college I had tried dating women. In seminary I didn't even try. Although two people I knew wrote theses on homosexuality, there was no discernible hint that it had personal meaning for them, and no one said, before an exchange of sexual interest, "I am one." In 1966 the topic was still unspeakable and the activity, as far as I knew, was something you did in the dark.

What is so extraordinary and painful, as I remember those years, is how unspeakable my feelings were. I remember two people I was very much in love with. I spent hours and hours talking about everything under the sun except what I was feeling toward them. I was best man for one of them, and cried as I left him and his bride in their honeymoon suite. When I finally got up the nerve to talk to the other one about my attraction to him, he immediately said we shouldn't see each other any more because obviously this was a disease. He had been trying to get rid of it for thirteen years in psychoanalysis, and it would be better for us not to "act it out." Seldom did I have sex with anyone who could talk about what we were doing and how we felt about it. In spite of my growing acquaintance with ordinary, successful and educated gay men, the real meaning for me of my homosexuality was in the dark and dingy theaters of Times Square.

Halfway through seminary, I was at a crisis point: I had in no way resolved my sexuality. I thought there was no place for me in life, much less the ministry, if I really lived a homosexual life style.

I took a year off from seminary and worked at a small New England college, teaching and directing the student union. During that year, I dated a woman, somewhat casually, and was satisfied to say goodbye until we spent several days together in the Maine woods at the end of summer, when I had sex with her for the first time. Another ecstatic experience! For three days I floated above the world! I was convinced this was a sign to me from God that my sexuality would be resolved, the doors of heterosexuality opened, and I could be a "normal" person. I returned to seminary, and we continued to date between Maine and New York.

I wanted a family desperately. I knew I wanted to be a father; I was less sure I wanted to be a husband. My former lover urged me to marry and have children if I could. When I went for psychotherapy to deal with my conflict, and the therapist said to me in a would-be enigmatic way, "Seek the first kingdom," I assumed this meant, "If you really love God, you'll marry."

So, one week before Stonewall, I got married and was ordained into the ministry in the United Church of Christ. Active first in the civil rights movement (which for me at that time meant black civil rights; I was only vaguely aware that it might have something to do with *my* rights as a gay man), then the anti-war movement, I sometimes used this as something I could feel unequivocally committed to, in contrast to the conflict I felt about my sexual urges, cries and longings. I discounted the body and certainly sexuality, telling myself that my petty desires were nothing compared with the real issues of napalmed babies in Vietnam. It was only when it came time to be absolutely on the front line as chair of Maine Clergy and Laity Concerned About Vietnam, that I trembled inside from a moral uncertainty. My heart was filled with shame: who can storm the barricades and lead others to do so when there is an ever-so-slight doubt: I am bad, so who am I to tell the government they're wrong? My shame about my homosexuality weakened my moral fortitude and clouded my confidence in my own judgment.

Over a period of years, I made all the right moves in upwardly-mobile parish changes, successful to the point of having two children, a station wagon, a golden retriever and vacations on the coast of Maine. Inwardly, I was a mess, constantly in emotional conflict, wanting to be somewhere I wasn't, with someone I wasn't, yet not willing to leave.

I tried to manage this conflict by drinking. From the very first, my anxiety over my relations with my wife was managed by Cutty Sark. The God of heterosexuality held forth in my life with the aid of some not-so-holy spirits. I drank to maintain outward appearance and squelch inner urges, to suppress feelings and have them. The more I tried to suppress my desire for men, the more I felt driven to seek men, often in potentially compromising and dangerous situations.

I loved family life. I loved my kids. I loved my wife, but not in the right way. So I felt like a total misfit; I was a stranger in a strange land, but no one knew except a couple of friends and my therapist. I was caught in a trap of my own making, but, like the monkey caught by holding onto rice in a coconut shell, I couldn't let go. I jogged around the Central Park reservoir feeling like I had to decide which arm to cut off, the right or the left, family or true self.

Finally, what had developed into alcoholism began to affect my work. I dreaded facing it, not just because I liked drinking, but because I knew that, having got into and sustained my marriage with the aid of these other spirits, if I gave them up I would have to face myself in a way I still had not done.

After ten years of marriage, within a single month, I told my wife I was alcoholic and gay. She didn't believe me and said I was just telling her things like that to upset her. She didn't want to face the truth any more than I did.

It still took awhile to decide that leaving the marriage was necessary. It took a long time for me to believe that I was okay enough, loved by God not only in spite of being gay, but in spite of breaking up the family. Finally, I came out and left the marriage because I was tired of being dead inside.

I had to change therapists and my notion of God. In my mind from the beginning, my marriage and ordination were linked: God was heterosexual-affirmative and homosexual-tolerant. Yet, when my therapist suggested that God would approve of me more if I stayed in my marriage, I knew he was wrong. Spelled out that baldly, I knew that was justification by works, and that if my childhood conversion experience meant anything, it meant God accepted me as I was, gay or straight, alcoholic or not, minister or not: unconditional grace. The polarity between my sexuality and spirituality had begun to revive: I was learning acceptance of my body, sometimes with the help of strangers, and I was learning a new, incarnational view of spirituality which affirmed my innate bodily urge to love. It was time to "let go and let God," to "turn the results over," and to accept other simplistic slogans which my intellectual orientation fought tooth and nail.

I was terrified of some legal barrier being placed between my daughters and me. I was afraid of losing job, community respect, professional support, love of all my family and friends—in sum, of winding up bereft and alone in the world. Fortunately, none of those fears of catastrophe have been realized, though the nature of all my relationships has deeply changed.

The hardest part, almost harder than the initial separation, was telling my daughters about my being gay. Coming out to anyone is always a test of the relationship; when it came to my own kids, I had to trust that they would still believe in the love they had already known more than the fears or prejudice that might be aroused. At the same time, I had to be ready to deal with a negative reaction from them. Except for this issue, however, we had a history of openness and honesty which was crucial. My secret was eating away at me, making me less available to them emotionally. "Dad, you seem preoccupied," my older daughter said that first Christmas Eve after the separation. After being so closeted for so long, I was not about to live the same way in the most important relationships of my life.

I sat them down and said, "I don't know whether you've picked it up or not, but there's something about myself that I want to tell you: that is, that I'm gay."

Both girls said they hadn't known anything and started crying. The eleven-year-old said, "Well you're my daddy and I love you anyway." The thirteen-year-old said, "I love you too, but I hope you won't embarrass me when I bring friends home, or kiss men on the street, or feel you have to make public speeches about gay lib, but on the other hand, you can't go back in the closet, so I guess you have a problem."

We continue to talk about the issue periodically as they go through their own coming-out process of having a gay dad. It has forced them into a deep level of consciousness not only about themselves and me, but about the dynamics of social prejudice of all kinds. Our relationship has in fact deepened and strengthened, not always smoothly, through this process. My younger daughter lives with me full-time, the older one part-time.

Coming out to the rest of my family met with more mixed results. My sister's first response was concern for how much pain I carried alone all those years before. She wished I could have shared it with her sooner. My mother consistently affirmed her love for me, but returned all the books I sent on the subject unread and refused to go to a PFLAG (Parents and Friends of Lesbians and Gays) group nearby.

A couple members of my extended family have always been racist as well as homophobic and sexist. My mother would tell me about such re-marks plaintively, as if she didn't know what to say. I wrote her back, reminding her that I had been raised all my life to be proud of my mentally and physically handicapped brother, and to defy anyone who ever looked the wrong way at him. During all that time, I told her, I carried within me the shame of knowing that there was no one in my family who would take a similar stand on my behalf in the face of anti-gay remarks, and now it was being proved true. I then sent letters coming out to my aunts, uncles and cousins. I got no response from any of them; it was as if all those letters had been swallowed up by the post office—or had never been sent. This silence, offering tolerance based on invisibility, blares out the truth of my position in the family: We only want you as we have known you; there never was a place for you as a gay person in this family and there never will be. However, the letter gave my mother the occasion she needed to confront others' homophobic remarks.

What is coming out like?

The peeling away of a banana to get at the succulent, hidden fruit?

The budding of a flower which nearly died from lack of water and sunlight?

No such niceties. For me, coming out has at best been like the peeling of an onion, as layer by layer of false selves, my fear-filled identities, my external validations, are pulled away until I wonder if there will be any me at the center. From a spiritual perspective, it has been an introduction to the refiner's fire.

I think it happened like this: In order to come out, personally and professionally, I had to be ready to stand alone, to declare who I am without waiting for others' approval. This seized autonomy, departing so from my entire previous way of living, set in motion the profoundest questions about who I am as a person that go far beyond my gay identity. To decide to live as a free, self-affirming person, is to subject every relationship, every commit-ment, allegiance, every assumed value and habit, to question.

I thought, when I confronted my alcoholism, that all I needed to do was stop drinking. When I came out, I thought all I needed to do was tell the truth about what I had been denying. In both instances, however, to take the matter seriously means, "How'd you like to change your life?" I was prepared for some rejection in the world. I didn't realize that coming out was the mere beginning of an internal revolution of a far greater magnitude than the outward changes.

Coming out means facing the central conflict within the self of the true, spontaneous, natural self that got buried in shame and lies underneath layers and layers of a false self erected to manage life in the outside world. It is therefore an exercise in consciousness-expansion in every direction.

Descent: Like diving for pearls, coming out requires going deep within to reclaim the true self that got buried, lost and denied. To get to it, you have to move through a lot of murky water, then mud, then crud. The murky water is the uncertainty, the lack of consciousness because of family's and church's and society's denial of the true self. To go through that murky water is to cut through and challenge everything you ever learned about who you are, which got confused with who you should be. The murkiness is the confusion between true self and false self. Pain and joy are the only touchstones; recovering the true self requires allowing oneself to feel again, because deep and true feeling was avoided.

There are also some guides into, and through, the murky waters: All those who have gone ahead in the reclaiming of lost selves—especially blacks and women—who, by words and examples, helped to lead the way. The downward ascent is a direct confrontation with one's internal authority; to get to the true self, it must be wrested from those to whom it was surrendered: mother, father, sister, brother, clubs, churches, professional groups, society, friends, et al. This internal confrontation affects, and is affected by, external relations in the outside world. The declaration of one's self as gay requires loyalty to a higher Self than the most intimate family connections (which are often threatened by the revelation); it is in service to the same higher loyalty of which Jesus spoke when he asked, "Who is my mother and who is my sister and brother?"

Busting, bursting out, breaking down, out forth. The decision to be who one is sets in motion changes on the horizontal level of external reality; likewise, changes on the external level set in motion the descent (some people start one place, some another; some are pushed by incidents, others are pulled by love, etc.). Confrontation with the internal authorities and the external authorities go back and forth, leading to fuller integration of internal and external self. This is where family crises, job crises, violence, breaking up of relationships, breaking down of all identities that were based on the false self, and the consequent awakening to one's unity with all oppressed people, happens. The self that one was becomes too small to contain all that one truly is. What had been an identity based on fear had created walls of fragile security that also set one apart from other marginalized people. This bursting the bounds of the false self, the collective identity, creates bonds with others who have suffered from systemic oppression. Sometimes this change, of course, is not chosen so much as it is suffered; one experiences a breakdown of old identities, old ways of being, that in fact is a falling apart; it is not really a "going crazy," however, as it is the failure of an old way of life making way for a new one.

Through work in Adult Children of Alcoholics and codependency, I have become aware of how inter-related my difficulty in coming out was with my origins in a dysfunctional family. I had buried not only my sexuality, but any sense of "I"-ness apart from what others needed me to be. What had seemed niceness and passivity was the repression of an entire feeling self, with dreams and hurts and angers too-long ignored, and a voice that was afraid to speak. Hidden amid resistance to my gayness and cloaked in professional care-taking was a resistance to my being anything other than the family role I had accepted, consisting primarily in being oriented toward others, with no apparent needs of my own. I began to see to what a global extent I had been trained to be "my brother's keeper," since I grew up taking care of him from his birth with cerebral palsy. I took care of others instead of having my own self; I thus rejected my own authority, rights and powers.

In collusion with family, church and society, I betrayed myself, and I have to take responsibility for my near-self-murder. To understand how this happened, I have to step outside those organizations and institutions, including my family, that rewarded me for my self-betrayal.

Debt was a fact of life in the closet where, because I wasn't free simply to be, I felt I deserved compensation, and so spent foolishly, ultimately going bankrupt. Losing my gold American Express card and all other good credit accoutrements has forced me to learn that I am enough "just as I am"—an old familiar tune. The shame involved in losing good credit status in this society pushed me to question the source of the shame, and led me into a radical critique of our consumer society.

Ascent. Parallel with the other movements, one discovers that the God one knew and gave allegiance to is too small. Combined, as that God was, with the false self and the collective identities, that God has to go. The vertical direction of the spiritual crisis has to be challenged: In fact, by whatever name—God, Goddess, Higher Power, Ground of Being, Transcendent Other or whatever—one's ultimate authority has to be confronted just like every other authority. We may even challenge the notion of vertical, of "looking up" to anyone or anything, and be forced to imagine new ways of relating to the More of our lives, to that which unites our true selves backward and forward in time and space. In this confrontation with the old, something new will be created that is crucially different from what went before: What is new will emerge from the assumption of the worth and validity of the true self, and the assumption that the true self's experience is a necessary resource in the construction of the new, rather than something to be denied and scorned. What is new will be both freer and scarier than the previous God, because that God was erected to give one a sense of control over life; the new emerges with letting go of such control, surrendering to a deeper and broader vitality.

Under conditions of alienation from my body, I tried to live as if it didn't count. As I began to challenge my inherited assumptions in theology and psychology, my body became a means of grace. A new poignancy was added to the words of the Eucharist, "This is my body. Take and eat....Take and drink." The Eucharist became sexual, and sex became holy in a way D. H. Lawrence and William Blake would have approved of. The reuniting of my split-off parts, the healing return of wholeness began.

Having already gotten one doctorate in pastoral counseling, I was stuck at this period in a would-have-been dissertation for a second one (another sign of my non-acceptance of myself). As I explored that stuckness, I discovered the profound extent to which, in my desperate need to make sure God was on my side, I had spent my entire life in a codependent relationship with God, preoccupied for forty plus years in trying to be a good boy, and trying not only to gain acceptance from God of my sexuality, but then trying to convince the church and society that being gay was okay with God too. I had spent my entire life, whether denying or affirming my homosexuality, trying to "get it right" vis-a-vis God, for fear that otherwise, the grace I had experienced as a child would no longer be there. While to most people this would appear to be simply good discipleship, it began to appear to me more clearly a case of being run by fear. A child who is truly confident of his parents' approval and love will not spend his time constantly asking for confirmation, but will, in that confidence, explore the world. This is precisely what I had not been able to do. I had spent my entire life trying to make sure I was doing the right thing. I didn't feel I had a self apart from the confirmations I got from the religious and professional establishment.

So I dropped out of the Ph.D. program and began to focus on whatever was coming up from within me, which turned out to be poems and stories. This feels much freer and more faithful to grace than the apologia I had been so chronically engaged in before.

What have I learned from my coming out experience?

I have learned that being yourself is the most difficult thing in the world, and that my mind is an indefatigable producer of diversions from my true self, thus confirming John Calvin's claim the human mind is a perpetual factory of idols.

I have learned that my gayness was only the tip of the iceberg of my fear-filled self, and that, once that was opened up, there was a host of other parts of myself—parts capable of greed, rage, pride, envy, sloth, etc., which did not conform to my carefully-cultivated-in-the-closet-nice-guy persona.

I have learned—the hard way, as they say—the power and privilege of credit card status: Without it, though you may leave home, the world does not recognize you as legitimate. In most places nowadays a driver's license with your picture on it is not enough to prove who you are; you aren't real until you are "backed up with a major credit card." Had I stayed in the closet, I would have continued along a much more socially acceptable path, and never learned the vicissitudes of living without credit. Internally, I have been able to see, by virtue of being on the other side, the extraordinary ways in which almost every social and interpersonal relationship is predicated on purchasing power, and how difficult it is to sustain relationships with a large discrepancy between people.

I have learned that finding and following your unique task—the thing to do which only you can do and without which the world will be just that much poorer—that finding and following is, like finding the true self, most difficult and subtle. It carries such fear with it that most people settle for economic and emotional comfort. To "follow your bliss," as Joseph Campbell urged, is extremely disquieting. Many of us gave up such hope long, long ago, and traded in creativity for survival.

How has my coming out affected my notion of, or relation to, God/ church/Christ/sacraments, etc.?

I resist my obligation to translate everything about my experience into Christian language and symbolism because that is precisely the felt obligation which I have assumed all my life and which is of the essence of codependency: Nothing is real until it is fitted into the pre-set formula to please a Parent. In codependency, my experience is never real, never valid in its own right, its own language, its own terms; it is only valid when it has been translated into, or analogies have been found with, the language and thought structure of the inherited tradition. The conclusion will always be some formulation of "Credo in unum deum, et filiis patris, et spiritus sanctus...et ecclesiam...." All new theology becomes apologetics; there is no kerygma. To assume the language and thought forms of the tradition and canon, and to make all subsequent experience contingent on that or deferential to what has gone before, is to lose the authority and power of the new and to retreat into safe stolidity.

I feel so wounded and betrayed by the years of service to and self-incrimination by, the heterosexual assumptions of Christian theology and the church, that, like an abused child, I am wary of all adults in authority, uncertain whether and whom to trust. The church which conveyed to me the message and experience of unconditional love simultaneously was my accuser, leaving me with the profoundest ambivalence about all things named "Christian." I based my entire life and all my fundamental decisions on the best knowledge and awareness I could muster; I took seriously the command to deny my self. I denied my basic impulses to serve what the church had defined (and still largely does) as good and valuable—i.e., to be heterosexually married forever—and learned only too painfully late that in so doing I had betrayed not only my self, but deceived those dearest to me. I feel jerked around, betrayed, toyed with and humiliated, a fool for having trusted.

It is not enough, therefore, to revise certain aspects of church ethics, especially about sexuality, or to say it's okay to be gay after all; there is something fundamentally wrong with a perspective that requires self-betrayal and surrender to a collective form of wisdom and authority for acceptance. This is the antithesis of grace. A radical winnowing is required, not merely the putting of a bit of new wine into old wineskins.

Let us begin by recognizing that the notion of God is a problem, not an easily-understood answer. God is a problem for me, on at least three levels: the metaphysical, the question of authority, and the patriarchal and sexist assumptions reflected in the very structure of traditional language.

1. On the metaphysical level, the problem was identified by Paul Tillich nearly forty years ago as the problem of theism: The only real God is not a being amid other beings, but is being-itself. This makes all naming of God, all addressing of God, irrespective of gender ascription, a misnomer, and all language that attributes personality, including personal agency, archaic, opening the field for everyone's personal or collective projection. To speak of or to God as if God were a person is necessarily to connect us to the internalized meanings from the church's exclusively heterosexual assumptions and to projections and transferences from our personal history—all of which must be articulated into consciousness. There is no free access to God by simple naming: To say "God" is to throw us into a complex of meanings and assumptions which must be carefully examined.

I believe that this is entirely biblical, consonant with Exodus 3:14, where YHWH eschews naming as a human attempt to pre-empt YHWH's freedom. The calling upon God as if "God" were a name, or a noun or pronoun or had an address, rather than being a symbol, makes us no more enlightened than totemists. Such language, in which key areas of our experience are projected out rather than identified within, leaves us disconnected from our bodies, the earth, other animals, the sky, and the sea. Such language necessarily brings us into what Tillich called the "subject-object scheme," in which God is one being among others. If God is not that, not one object among others, then how is speech to or about God possible? The debate about God's gender amid such a question seems to me like the shifting of chairs on the Titanic. I am no more interested in calling God mother than I am in calling God father. We must recover the no-thing-ness of God. No spirituality or theology will work for me that does not honor—IN THE WAY IT USES LANGUAGE—the utter transcendence of God. I do not know if it is even fitting to ascribe action or motivation or intention to God; I am not sure that there is any cosmic intention in the universe or that being is headed toward, or in the service of, anything except its own becoming.

2. In order to initiate the revolution toward self-acceptance, we gay

people have had to deeply value our personal experience, to learn to value our innermost feelings, intuitions, perceptions and longings, and to value this experience as more determinative than any external authority. No speech about God, therefore, can be meaningful unless it is deeply rooted in personal experience. No concept of God can be authoritative that does not derive from our experience both of suffering and unconditional acceptance. All speech, therefore, that suggests a premature bending of the knee, or a worship of something beyond what we have personally experienced as true, is suspect. What is authoritative is not something "out there," neither a concept of deity, nor in writings which, by having survived a group process, are called canon and dogma, nor in a male-dominated institution. What is authoritative is the reality of our own experience, especially our experience of that peculiar brand of unconditional acceptance in the face of suffering and oppression which we call grace.

3. This brings us to the level of associated patriarchal and sexist meanings to God language. In order to affirm my gayness as a primary mode of being in the world, claiming my particular mode of attraction, awareness and sensibility, I have had to expand my understanding of God. And what is expanded is not simply a new inclusive slot for gay people, following, however, so slowly behind slots for women, African-Americans and other "minorities," so-called by the white people who wrote most of what we call Christian tradition. Instead of a hierarchy with ascending and descending levels of being and concomitant notions of more/less, better/worse, higher/lower—notions that serve to rank human differences—we need to see, accept and affirm the entire panoply of differences in creation—the notion not of hierarchy into which we may now count ourselves invited on a subordinate scale, but an inexhaustible variety of human modes of being, perceiving, creating and experiencing.

I have been forced by my gay experience to confront not only sexism and heterosexism, but patriarchy as a whole. It is patriarchy that feels compelled to control sexuality and to subject all people to sexist and heterosexist males. Witness the most recent threats of excommunication to people supporting abortion rights. We must question our every impulse to put something—some idea, notion, concept—into the emptiness of being-itself. Recent physics, as always, is suggestive: Just as there is no irreducible matter, but only clusters of energy in different forms, so there is no "god," no object, no personality, beyond what theologian John MacQuarrie said we are brought to, namely, "being has the character of grace."

I will always be a Christian in the same way that I will always speak English. I may learn other languages, but English is my native tongue and all others will be secondary, learned, rather than part and parcel of my brain and blood and bones. Similarly, I will never be able to think in other terms as spontaneously and naturally as Christian ones: My entire psyche and soul is Christian-language-structured. I cannot not think this way. Creation, redemption, crucifixion, resurrection, eucharist, incarnation, Jesus, body, blood—these words will always carry a certain energy for me—and with it, the assumptions about the universe.

I am a Christian: I believe in the crucifixion and the resurrection as polarities of human existence. I believe in the death of the ego as prerequisite to the birth of the new self; I believe in the incarnation of God's very beingness in the midst of the weakest and lowliest of creatures, and the ultimate failure of injustice (more than I believe in the triumph of righteousness). I believe in the sacrament of holy communion, the veritable presence of salvation in the biting into and swallowing of our brokenness, the opening of the self to love beyond our own fear of love. I believe in the virgin birth as signifying the possibility of innocence, new beginnings, amid our otherwise calcified defenses, i.e., our sin, our self-made poisons, our prisons and destructions.

But to get to the point where, after all the demythologizing, deconstructing and decoding, all this comes alive, is not only tiresome and ennervating, but makes me wonder whether the entire enterprise isn't too misguided, too far off base to bother with.

What is my alternative? Humanism? No, not if by that one infers a one-dimensional view of humankind, a final reliance on reason. I believe the world is sustained, if it is at all, by God. But we can't talk about God very well, nor very much; silence and meditation, much self-reflection, and much being known by compassionate and fearless others is required.

I have not gone to church for some time. It does not seem to address my spiritual needs as I understand them, in spite of my local church being strongly gay-affirmative. My spiritual needs are mostly met in personal meditation, social protest, writing, self-care (such as massage, personal therapy, swimming, walking on beaches or in woods) and conversations with people who seem to share my journey.

As I review the last few years' events, and the unlayering of my identities as a heterosexual, married, upwardly mobile parish minister complete with credit lines, I know that what has been lost has been prerequisite to gain. Though I cannot say I "have a self" in the way Kierkegaard meant, I do believe I am no longer denying the self that is seeking its true form.

Inwardly, I feel like I have entered a cloister, exchanging a clerical collar and a therapist's tie for a monk's robe and a vow of silence, if not chastity. In a paradoxical way, the recovery of my own self and voice has led me to an inner silence and listening, rather than speaking. Who I am and

where I am going is less clear now than at any other point in my life.
And that is just fine.

Robert W. Gunn, D.Min., a child of southern Illinois, a teenager in Florida, a bedazzled Columbia student in the Emerald City, a pastor in the Maine woods, Boston and Long Island, is currently a pastoral psychotherapist in private practice in New York City. He is on the faculty of the pastoral counseling department of the Postgraduate Center for Mental Health. As a Fellow in the American Association of Pastoral Counselors, he is on the Association's Regional Theological and Social Concerns Committee and initiated the Caucus on Lesbian, Gay and Bisexual Concerns. He enjoys playing the piano, singing and scuba diving.

M.R. RITLEY
Set Apart, Called into the Midst

S eptember 1985. Dead ahead of me, the stained glass window that soars up behind the altar is a blaze of fractured crimson, splintered reds and scarlets: the colors of fire, blood and spirit. The strong male voices of the Gay Men's Chorus fill the church with the Lotti Mass in B Flat Minor. All around me, packing the church, are the faces of men and women I have known for years, but never seen in a church before. I wonder if they are as startled to me here, dressed like an overgrown altar boy, as I am to see them. I take my place at the head of the procession, before the cross and torches, waiting for the signal to begin the slow, majestic journey toward the altar. This is the second AIDS Mass I have served at, bringing the one gift that I can offer here: I can swing a thurible like no three people in the state. And today I have been asked to pull out all the stops: This is a celebration most particularly gay, particularly ours.

I am here because I have my own beloved dead, whose lives I want to celebrate, but even more than that, I have come to recognize an aching silence: century after century of silent lives, the men and women we should have celebrated, but whose names and lives are lost to us for all time in the void where gay history ought to be. Today, at least, one person will remember them.

The master of ceremonies nods for me to begin, and I start slowly down the nave. This is what I came here to do. Timing my movement to the music, I send the thurible sweeping up and around in a 360-degree arc, all glitter and smoke—once, twice, three times—my silent offering to those silent lives, a gesture as gay as the woman who makes it. I am celebrating the queens I knew who would have loved it: Cyr and Ronnie, Kai and Lesley. Celebrating, too, the women in whose place I stand. I may be silent, but this is not an ordinary acolyte in front of the procession: This is a cross-dressed woman come to grieve and celebrate her people.

This moment has somehow come to epitomize my whole life: It has all come together in this scene. Here I am, a gay woman, dead-center in the liturgy, an inextricable part of this ceremony. To all outward appearances I am completely a part of this place, a visible member of the church, enacting its most central ritual.

And in reality? I have lived the last eighteen months as a pariah in this parish, as isolated and alone as if I were in the middle of the desert. I have been lied about, my character and integrity have been slandered; I have been shown in no uncertain terms that I am persona non grata here. Yet Sunday after Sunday I have vested and stood in the sanctuary, serving those who serve at the altar, sometimes seeing icy hatred in the eyes of people who don't even know me. Each Sunday I take the cross and lead the procession in at the start of the service; then I go into the back of the church and place it carefully in its holder, walk outside and stand on the patio until after the exchange of the peace, when I go in and serve during the eucharist. My presence in the congregation would be a lie, and I cannot bear it. And yet I go on doing it, and I refuse to leave. I did not come this far to be done in now, and nothing on earth will make me retreat.

It has been a long and roundabout journey, and if I have come to know anything at all about God, it is a God who is a fellow traveler, a God who has led me, followed me, and sometimes merely staggered with me through impossible and barren desert places. I started out believing that God was what I was searching for. I have come to find, in these last few months, that God has rather been my fellow-seeker, and that somehow my quest is exactly what God needs of me: That I companion God in this journey, to reach whatever it is that God and I together journey toward.

But it has been a very long and risky trip.

SET APART

I was nurtured and defined by the spiritual ferment of the '60s, my thinking and my life shaped by the forces of the counter-culture. For a gay woman, well aware that she would never fit the patterns of mainstream culture, it was a heady and creative time. Black, gay, Native American, flower child and peacenik, we turned our lives and values upside-down in a riot of the senses, an overwhelming conviction that we were, somehow, creating a new world, where power, peace and freedom were to have new meanings.

For me, also, it was the first time I had words to define myself, the vocabulary of gay liberation when gay liberation meant a spiritual awakening: *Gay is a spiritual quality. We are a separate people, and we have the right to be.*

It was not a time when the church's word had any credibility: What it had said about me was a lie, and with that lie it had forfeited the right to speak to me, for me, to define me or condemn me. Shorn of the images of God I had been raised with, I found myself in an exhilarating, scary, uncharted new world of the spirit, pregnant with possibilities, mined with unexpected pitfalls. I gravitated to a spiritual discipline that spoke to my condition: a desert way, a way of emptying oneself, of struggle, doubt and inner discipline. But a way shot through with the luminous vision of the Sufi mystics, at times an overpowering sense of God's presence. The practice was simple, all-consuming:

> Go where you are sent.
> Wait till you are shown what to do.
> Do it with the whole self.
> Remain till you have done what you were
>   sent to do.
> Walk away with empty hands.

It was my life, a life in which I discovered an unexpected treasure trove of gifts. I became a teacher, a preacher, a spiritual leader, a woman who began to see herself as a crucible in which ideas took shape, in which the very stuff of abstraction could be given life, form, put into words that moved and touched others. I thought: This is what I was born to do, this pays for everything. Out of my own lostness, I have somehow helped others find their way; out of my own imprisonment I have somehow become a doorway through which others can walk into freedom. And underlying that, the conviction that no one walks out alone, that no one makes the journey all alone, and that somehow our separate struggles are caught up in a larger movement toward—what? I wasn't sure. I wasn't sure at all.

Was it in God that I needed to find the answer? Or was it in a deeper understanding of my humanness, the very commonality of our struggles, that extended beyond the borders of "gay" and "straight," yet somehow gave peculiar meaning to my gayness.

Caught up in the ferment of that incredible decade, I began to move toward a formulation of my own. I gestated it, I gave it shape, I taught it. It is very much a part of me even now. It underlies the greater part of my journey, and my conviction about people (especially gay people) and God. It is this:

THE RIFT IN THE MYTHIC FABRIC

We are, as creatures, peculiarly frail, utterly incomplete. Of all the creatures in the known world, we alone are born *without a single natural way of life*. We are incomplete in instinct and capacity. Tigers and foxes, wart-hogs and the lowly tree toad, are all born better equipped by nature than are we: Each has a natural way of life, whether predator or ruminant, a natural role spelled out for them in terms of climate, diet, mating and nesting patterns. We alone have no such natural pattern to achieve. We build cultures out of the same need that makes a beaver build dams, or swallows a nest: because we cannot survive without them. We are as easily tribal as familial, as readily carnivorous as vegetarian, as frequently aggressive as pacifistic.

Engrave this on your mind: *There is no natural way of life for human beings.* All are equally creations of the human mind and spirit, improvisations, inventions, the stuff of imagination brought to bear on the task or surviving in a given world.

And therein lies the clue to the one natural thing about the way we live at all: It is our nature to create, as well as our need to create a pattern within which we can live at all. We alone cannot live naked in the environment, but of necessity must clothe ourselves in the subtle stuff of word and symbol, myth and meaning. Shatter the symbols, rob us of meaning, and we become ill, whether as a culture or an individual.

God, if you like, not only gifted us with the capacity to grow, to discover, to create: This same god provided us with an endless need to do so. This is God's ironic way with us—that every gift is also a need. Our mastery of the environment is not an evidence of human superiority, but of our endless vulnerability and incompleteness. We are far more frail than the world we live in. Trees can easily outlive us; even dandelions are tougher. It is out of our very frailty that we evoke our greatest gifts.

All visions of reality are by their nature mythic, constructions we super-impose on what would otherwise be a chaos of event and gesture. Myth is the lens we look through, the means we use to define the shape of the world we see. And the more closely the world we see conforms to the outlines of the myth, the less mythic we regard it as being. Instead, we say simply, "But that's the truth. This is the way it really is."

We might say, then, that a myth derives its power, in part, from the fact that it is a reasonably accurate description of the way life is experienced. For the well-entrenched sixth-generation Anglo, who occupies a position of power and whose life is cushioned by enough economic and social resources to make it an affirmative, orderly existence, the American myth is no myth at all, but the way things obviously are. The world conforms to the dimensions of the myth.

The question is: What happens when life, as experienced by most people, does not conform to the shape of the myth that undergirds it, when the ripples in the lens, as it were, get out of sync with the world viewed through it? It happens, historically, has happened many times. A rift appears in the mythic fabric, and the underlying structure begins to part until it gives way entirely.

These periods, when the mythic rift is taking place, are peculiarly full of energy, times of intense, and often erratic, new visions—and equally, of violence, insanity and social disruption. For when the lens we look through is shattered, the world loses its shape. Even more profoundly, the myth is also the lens through which we see and define ourselves, and the slightest crack in it is experienced as life-threatening. We resist it as fiercely as we would resist having an arm or leg lopped off, for we instinctively know that we are losing the very center of the self. Make no mistake about it: People whose mythic view of life is undergoing this kind of dislocation are people in enormous fear and pain. They must be dealt with as compassionately—and as warily—as an animal with its leg in a trap. They are frightened, and they can be dangerous. But their fear and their danger does not make them any less in need of help.

Always, it is in those areas that have fallen outside the boundaries of the previous mythic world-view, that the new mythic equation emerges. The emerging middle class had no place in the medieval social synthesis, that well thought out picture of the cosmos with its fixed boundaries and classes. It erupted into the collapsing world of the late medieval synthesis, formulating its own mythic view, and played it out in the fields of religion, politics and economics. It is no coincidence that nationalism, capitalism and the Reformation found their most energetic formulators in that previously unclassed class. It is one age's disenfranchised who can most easily see through the myth, and create the mythic structure of the next age.

What can we say about the world we live in now, if not that it is a world in which the myth is increasingly out of sync with the reality experienced by a larger and larger number of people? We are in the midst of just exactly such a massive psychic dislocation, one of the watershed periods when the organizing myth that has undergirded Western life for better than five centuries is not only beginning to tear, but has already ruptured deep under the surface.

And who are we, as gays, if not a people for whom the myth was never anything but myth, who always fell outside the boundaries of its reality? Gays and women, blacks and third-worlders, we are the ones out of whose experience of life new images are being born, because they are the images that describe the world we really know, articulate the pains and exultation of what it means to be who we are, give shape and definition to the journeys we have made.

It is ours to do, the gift we have to offer, even to a world that does not want it. Because in deeper terms, the world that does not want it desperately needs it if it is to survive at all.

God from whose unimaginable imagination the whole cosmos was called into being, you have given us such power! You call out to us in the deepest reaches of imagination: "Name me, call me into your lives in a thousand images. I will reply, I will respond: I will fill them with meanings beyond your power to imagine."

CALLED INTO THE MIDST

Ironically, I learned only too well how true this all was. Because, as I neared my forties, it was my own myth that began to shatter, my own vision that splintered into a chaos of terrifying meaninglessness. In one single, bitter year, it was all swept away: my community, my career, my sense of who I was and what I was about, even, for a long and agonizing time, my sense of God. It was as if a hole had been ripped out of the center of the universe, and I had fallen into that vast emptiness, and kept falling, falling....

The next several years were an agonizing struggle with mental darkness, a struggle that used up all my energy. I can remember sitting on the edge of the bed, crying helplessly because I did not have the strength to put on my shoes and walk out my apartment door. I learned that despair was easily as powerful as anger, and that it had to be wrestled, fought into the ground each morning before I could get up and face another day. I survived somehow in this vacuum, this space that once had held a life.

On the day before my fortieth birthday, I wandered into a church building looking for a 12-Step meeting I desperately needed to attend. I got lost. Wandering around looking for an exit, I found myself in the empty church, in the choir behind the altar, looking out across the altar at an enormous, blazing window in which, in fragmented colors, was the figure of Christ.

I was horrified and thought, "Oh, shit! How the hell do I get out of here?" I headed for the doors at the other end of the church.

I was stopped half way, as if I had walked into a wall, by an overwhelming sense of the presence that had disappeared into the unbearable vacuum three years before. I can only describe it like being suddenly immersed in love. In the center of this bewildering warmth, this sense of presence, it was as if everything distilled into a single word: *Here*, M. R. *Here*.

And a decade and a half of spiritual discipline asserted itself. Go where you are sent. Wait till you are shown what to do. Do it with the whole self. Remain till you have done what you were sent to do. Walk away with empty hands.

But *here?* Why on earth here? This is not my world; I don't belong here. I've lived in a world so different from the one these people know that I might as well have been on another planet. I'm not even a person any more, only a box of spare parts. I'm barely functional.

And besides, I'm gay.

I ran.

I struggled against this for nearly four months, in a war of attrition: on one side, God's seductive presence and my own fiercely instilled spiritual discipline; on the other side, my feelings, in complete revolt and panic. I was well aware that I was being asked to enter a world whose language I did not even know, whose worship was an utter mystery to me, whose social norms I not only didn't share, but didn't even understand. I was asked to enter it as a woman only nominally functional, still so shaky in her recovery that I could barely carry on a conversation, barely tolerate the company of strangers. I had been known to abandon my shopping cart in the middle of the produce section and flee because I had become aware that there were six other people in the market. And I was being asked to go.

I went. Warily, grudgingly, carrying the full freight of my fractured personality, hanging on for grim life to the only thing I knew: Go where you are sent. Wait till you are shown what to do.

I went, trying to fathom this God who had called me, how different, how like the God I understood before. The language, the symbols, the ritual were as opaque to me as Swahili. And I hadn't the strength to try to make bridges, hadn't the courage to risk being fractured again. Until, one Sunday morning, Malcolm Boyd preached a sermon that contained three lines that all but seared me:

> Burnt-out people
> play with fire again,
> light candles in darkness.

I understood. I had come where I was sent. I had now to wait till I was shown what to do. And somehow, burnt-out, fractured, broken beyond my own bearing, I would find a way to do it with the whole self. I was afraid. I was downright petrified. But I consented.

I did not know what I believed. But I knew what I did not believe, and slowly, by following the trail of disbelief, I began to find a very tenuous strip of ground on which to stand. I did not believe the God who called me into being created me without a reason. I did not believe that in making me this God had merely made a defective hetero. I believed with all my heart that, yes, God set me apart—set us apart, created us a separate people, and intended us to be a separate people.

Why God had gifted me with gayness I could certainly not say, and in fact it became harder and harder to define to myself exactly what "gay" was. It was not so much a thing of body as of spirit, a way of being. I knew that even among gays I was part of a minority: I did not believe that we were "just like everyone else." I believed we were profoundly different, common in our humanness, but utterly distinct. But how would I define that diffe. ence? We cannot be identified as a minority because of color, genitalia or nation. We alone, of all minorities, are a people defined by our loves.

I did not believe that a God who created me to express a particular kind of love had anything but love in mind in making me so. I did not believe that God conferred my gayness on me as a flaw, but as a gift. And yes, like every gift, it was also a need. Having been born by the grace of God gay, having lived as a gay woman in a gay world, I had a gift—and I needed to give it. And here, exactly here, was where I was being asked to give it.

A SEPARATE PERSON WITH A SEPARATE VOICE

It did not take a form I would have chosen. My parish became, in a very short time, a kind of battleground where gender was the line along which our community divided. The center of the storm was the question of inclusive language, but the underlying turmoil was the rage of women who had only just discovered that they had bought a myth, a myth that ultimately crippled them.

I felt curiously distanced from all this. I had spent most of my life in the gay subculture, where I was a self-defining entity. We were not only products of different cultures, but we apparently experienced gender quite differently. To them, it was the ultimate dividing line of reality. They were women: The others were men. They knew perfectly well what side of the line everyone belonged on. For me, however, gender has always been a tenuous thing at best—its edges blur in me, lose their sharp distinction in my own androgynous and double-natured self. Western culture has only two words for gender, only two pronouns—and neither fits me.

And so I floundered, a woman immersed in the visible life of my church, but completely isolated at its center, set apart by differences so deep my language did not even have the words for it. I almost gave up. But I was asked to serve at the first AIDS Mass, and reluctantly I agreed. It was that service that began to turn my life around. I was here because I was gay, because I stood in the sanctuary for all those gay brothers who could not stand here, all those gay sisters who had left here out of loneliness as deep as mine. And somehow, in the breaking of the bread, the pouring of the wine, the pieces of my life were gathered up into a whole I had not known existed. I felt as if it were I who somehow had been offered here.

Dear God, I prayed, you made me whole, at least as male as female.

Somehow, in this headiest, most perilous of all your gifts, you enclosed in this single-gendered body a double-gendered spirit, a person who was meant to be native to both sides of the equation. All my life I've had to struggle to hang onto both sides of myself: I will not choose, I will not choose, I will not hate either half of me, even if it makes me alien to both men and women. I will not give up either half because it would be the ultimate betrayal of your gift to me. I will go on believing that you called me here exactly and precisely because I am gay, a separate person from a separate people. You called me into the midst of these people, these others, for a reason.

No one walks out alone, and somehow, every one of us was meant to be a door for others. For whatever unfathomable reason, you enter our lives only where we choose to open a door, or where—when life has damaged us—a hole has been torn. Like the birth of myth, you erupt through the rift where the fabric of the self is torn. And if I let you enter through the broken fabric of my life, perhaps—maybe just perhaps—I can become one of the broken places through which you can enter the life of the whole. But how? How?

God who called me into being, what power have you given me? You go on calling, sometimes pleading: "Name me, call me into your world in a thousand images. I will reply, I will respond: I will fill them with meaning beyond your power to imagine."

How would a double-gendered woman speak to an infinitely-gendered God? How would a woman from a people defined by love define the one who defined the very stuff of love? What would a gay prayer sound like, a prayer from someone whose first line of self-acceptance is: I am a sexual being. I love in a given way, and nothing on earth can stop me from loving this way. And I will, by God, even love God this way!

I prayed. And I began to write a prayer, a eucharist to celebrate all the parts of myself and my people that had been left outside. In many ways, the prayer wrote me at the same time. I brought it with me to one of those angry, angry meetings on inclusive language. And the anger was somehow drowned in the wash of its power. I took it to a Lenten study group on sexuality and spirituality, and I was dumbfounded by its impact. No one noticed that it spoke of neither "he" nor "she." They only heard one pronoun: "You."

And one Sunday in May 1986, we celebrated it at the principal service, at the altar I had first seen as a stranger, lost in the building and looking for a 12-Step meeting. I had gone where I was sent. Now I would have to leave the rest to God.

I had wanted to be the acolyte that day, to stand in the sanctuary where I had been so terribly alone, while my prayer was spoken. I handed up the paten and the chalice to the subdeacon, received the wine and the water from the deacon when the chalice had been filled, washed the celebrant's hands. But none of those were the reason I was there. God's reason for calling a gay woman into the midst of this congregation was shaped in the air with the celebrant's first words:

The Great Thanksgiving

In this prayer, the lines in italics are spoken by the People.

Celebrant
May God be with you.

People
And also with you.

Celebrant
Give God your hearts.

People
We give our hearts to God, and to each other.

Celebrant
Let us celebrate our love for God.

People
As we celebrate God's love for us.

Celebrant
Heart of the universe, giver of all gifts, Life who loves us into being, we are your lovers, your people, who come together to celebrate your gifts to us. Be with us, join us, as we lift our voices, giving thanks and singing,

Celebrant and People
Holy, holy, holy One, God of power and might,
heaven and earth are full of your glory.
   Hosanna in the highest.
Blessed is the One who comes in the name of our God.
   Hosanna in the highest.

Celebrant
Holy and gracious God, out of love you created the universe, and filled it with the treasure of your limitless imagination, breathed the splendor and the terror of the storm, the breathless silence of the moment just before the

dawn. You called forth life in all its billion forms, delicate beyond belief and stunning in its majesty and strength.

Out of love, you called us into being, called us to share the wonder of creation with you, gave us your power to love and create, the gift of your desire and your imagination.

You have blessed us with a million lovely and delicious stirrings of our senses: new-mown grass and autumn's burning; the nursing infant's mouth against our breast; the stinging cold of mountain air; a kiss before sleep.

You have felt it with us, celebrated it, delighted with us in the wonders of the senses you created. You are the one who touches us, who feels with us, who shares our pleasure.

You have given us your passion to embrace life and embody it, the strength and grace of bodies animated with your spirit: Bodies that have danced and fought and loved with us, shared our labors and our pleasures with us. Bodies that brought us into life, and through which we have given birth.

Dear God, we have been ashamed, afraid, unloving to ourselves; we have turned away from this great lover's gift to us, his miracle of strength and beauty. Help us to love our bodies, cherish them, and give our thanks to you through them.

You have looked at us with eyes that asked us only for our love: the eyes of a black child who will never live to see your wonders, the eyes of our gay brother who has always stood outside, the eyes of a woman bowed with the tragedies of loss and war, whose only language is her tears, eyes that have asked us only for compassion.

How often we have turned away, have left your cry for love unheeded. Yet even as we turned aside you looked at us with love in the eyes of those who cared, who touched us, and restored our hearts.

You have loved life so deeply, so fearlessly, that you—our Lover and our God—embraced this life of ours, embodied it, became one of us, to share our life with us and give us yours. You came to us with a newborn's helplessness, grew up among us, grieved our dead with us and danced at our weddings. You touched us when we were untouchable, and healed us when we had no hope.

You knew the darkest secrets of our hearts, and yet you went on loving us, and helping us to love ourselves. Even in the face of fear, and fear's power to destroy life, you went on loving us.

Celebrant and People

On that last night when we sat together at the table, you took bread in the hands you had worked with, touched us with. You broke it, thanking God for the gift of bread and the hands that had made it. You said" "Here: Take, eat. This is my body. I give it out of love for you. Do this, and remember me always."

When we had shared our meal, you took the cup of wine, and you blessed God for the vineyard and the grapes, the wine pressed out for us by human hands. You touched it to us and said: "Drink this. This is my very life's blood, which I shed for you and for all, to heal you and make you whole. Whenever you gather together, do this, and remember me."

We have remembered you, and what you were to us. We remember also: That you died, and that from death you rose again to life, and that you promised us that you would come again, to be with us forever.

Celebrant

God, who has worn a thousand faces—Father, Mother, Lover, Friend—we have remembered, and we offer you these gifts, this bread and wine, to share once more your life and spirit. Bless them, and be present in them. Let them be once more your body, freely given into life and death, your blood, shared with us in the mystery of healing and unending life. Bless these lives and bodies that we bring to you, and fill us with your presence, that your life may be our lives, your spirit ours.

We ask this for the sake of the love that we have shared, and in remembrance of your promise.

And now, as you have taught us, we say together,

Our God in heaven,
> *hallowed be your Name,*
> *your kingdom come,*
> *your will be done,*
>> *on earth as it is in heaven.*
Give us today our daily bread.
Forgive us our sins
> *as we forgive those who sin against us.*
Save us from the time of trial,
> *deliver us from evil.*
For the kingdom, the power,

and the glory are yours,
now and for ever. Amen.

The Breaking of the Bread

The Celebrant breaks the consecrated Bread. A period of silence is kept.

Alleluia. Christ our Passover is sacrificed for us;
Therefore let us keep the feast. Alleluia.

Celebrant
The Gifts of God for God's Beloved People. Take them, remembering
that Christ died for you, and let Christ nurture you within, through love and
faith.

The Communion

After Communion, the Celebrant says

Let us pray.

Celebrant and People
Eternal God, our Lover and Creator,
You have gifted us, and made us living members
of our Savior Jesus Christ;
You have fed us and sustained us
with Christ's Body and Blood.
Be our strength and courage
as we go into your world
to love and serve and find you,
and fill us with your grace
through Christ our Savior and Redeemer. Amen.

The Celebrant then blesses the people, and dismisses them with these
words

Let us go forth in the name of Christ.

People
Thanks be to God.

* * *

The deacon (who was gay) wept at the altar. Throughout the church I could see faces that mirrored the power of the words. Something had touched living flesh here, living spirit. This is what I came here to do: I came to speak in a voice that is neither man nor woman but both, to speak for the part of every man and woman here who is their own walled-out and stranger self. Dear God, you gave me—gave us—the power to articulate this, because we have been given the burden of knowing what it feels like, and the incredible strength of spirit to transform it from burden to gift. In this fractured congregation, which can no longer bear its very differences, make me a bridge, throw me across the chasm like a rope! Even flung out to hang in empty space, make me a foothold for others. I'm not afraid of the perilous place between the worlds: It's my native land, I've lived there all my life. And I have known your presence in the emptiness.

The bread was broken, the wine was poured. Standing at the credence table waiting to put away the empty chalices, the words of a Sufi teacher suddenly came back to me: "This is why you do it, why you go on. You are to make yourself bread for God's banquet. God has given you the wheat and water, and life has given you the leavening. Now all you need do is pass through the fire." At the time I had first heard it, I knew I hadn't the courage to do it, and I grieved. But now, I was overwhelmed with a rush of blazing gratitude and humility. I had walked through the fire. And God was humble enough to receive my gift, to take the offered bread, to make me part of the banquet.

It was one of the moments I loved the best: the quiet moment at the end of the service, when the sanctuary was empty, and I went in alone to put the candles out, a gay woman offering this final silent service. When I turned, one of the women who had understood my struggles over the last year, who had more than once seen my tears, more than once given me the courage to go on, appeared at the altar rail. A woman whose world was not at all like mine, a woman with a family, with children and grandchildren, who nevertheless had shared my journey, she simply embraced me now. I felt exhausted, drained, and could only say, "I think today was what I came here to do." And she nodded, holding my hands in hers, and said, "You came to us a stranger, and you learned to speak our language. And now you've spoken to us in it."

It paid for everything.

Wayfaring God, sharer of the journey, of all the gifts you gave us, surely this is the richest: You made us a separate people, born by the grace of God gay, and gifted with the power of unquenchable love. You set us apart as a people defined by our loves, and then, in love's baffling fashion, you called us into the midst of your people, where our brokenness becomes the door through which you enter. You gave us the wheat and the water, but the leavening is ours. We have walked through the fire. Now, out of love for us, grant us the greatest gift that we can ask of you: Take this bread, and feed the hearts that hunger still.

M. R. Ritley has had what she describes as a "spiritually adventurous" life. Raised in an ethnic community in Cleveland, Ohio, she has been a Californian for many years. For more than a decade she was a teacher, writer and spiritual director in a non-Western spiritual tradition, later worshiped with the Religious Society of Friends (Quakers), and eventually became a member of the Episcopal Church.

In addition to many years of involvement in publications, she is the author of several experimental textbooks in the social sciences, and has been a lecturer on cultural history, psychohistory and religion. She is currently studying theology at the Graduate Theological Union in Berkeley, California, and is working on a book integrating Sufi spiritual disciplines and Christian spirituality.
